Creating Curb Appeal

Michelle Valigursky & Lisa Vail

Schiffer Publishing Ltd

4880 Lower Valley Road Atglen, Pennsylvania 19310

Primary Photography by
Theresa M. Grant

Dedication

To Ed, Mike, and Nick,
for being my greatest
supporters and biggest
fans. I love you, always.
M.V.

To George, for standing by
me. And for Haven and
Jordan, my beautiful girls.
L.V.

To Dad, for teaching me
the Sunny 16 Rule. And
for both Mom and Dad,
for always being there.
T.M.G.

Copyright © 2009 by Michelle Valigursky and Lisa Vail
Photos © 2009 by Theresa M. Grant unless otherwise noted
Library of Congress Control Number: 2009925853

ISBN: 978-0-7643-3278-4
Designed by "Ellen Taltoan"
Type set in Zurich BT/Dutch809 BT
Printed in China

Published by Schiffer Publishing Ltd.
4880 Lower Valley Road
Atglen, PA 19310
Phone: (610) 593-1777; Fax: (610) 593-2002
E-mail: Info@schifferbooks.com

For the largest selection of fine reference books on this and related subjects, please visit our web site at:
www.schifferbooks.com
We are always looking for people to write books on new and related subjects. If you have an idea for a book please contact us at the above address.

This book may be purchased from the publisher.
Include $5.00 for shipping.
Please try your bookstore first.
You may write for a free catalog.
In Europe, Schiffer books are distributed by
Bushwood Books
6 Marksbury Ave.
Kew Gardens
Surrey TW9 4JF England
Phone: 44 (0) 20 8392 8585; Fax: 44 (0) 20 8392 9876
E-mail: info@bushwoodbooks.co.uk
Website: www.bushwoodbooks.co.uk

Contents

Functional necessities like light posts take on presence when surrounded by resplendent blooms -- though be sure not to obscure house numbers.

Accessories can be meaningful as well as functional. *Photo by Michelle Valigursky*

When placing a fountain, position seating for ideal enjoyment. *Photo by Michelle Valigursky*

Preface

As a little girl with a dad in marketing, and now with a husband in sales, I've moved every few years of my life. I've enjoyed new schools, new friends, new jobs, and 17 new homes in six states. Each time, the process is the same. I begin with a quiet introduction to my new home and community. As I settle my family, I slowly get to know my new space, to understand its nuances and its needs.

Each of my homes expresses its own personality. In Connecticut, one charming yellow Cape Cod was bounded by a century-old fieldstone wall, while another salt box Colonial stood proud on a boulder-strewn yard. A New Jersey 1960s split level boasted Mediterranean double doors and a moon shaped patio, while another cottage was surrounded by pale climbing roses. In Maryland farm country, where winters were harsh and lovely, our glassy contemporary house overlooked a golf course wonderland of snow-covered fairways and cherry trees. And now in Georgia, my brick traditional home sits high on a sloping wooded acre, perched above a flowing stream and dogwood-dappled greenery.

My philosophy is simple: *love where you live.* Embrace a home's strengths and alleviate its weaknesses through creative problem solving and innovative applications. Express yourself, even in the smallest ways, to claim a property as your own and leave your signature behind.

I've lived in homes of many styles and take with me to each new residence an appreciation for all types of architecture and design. With each moving-in challenge, I draw elements from the home styles of my past and study examples of great properties nearby to create a well-balanced, inspirational presentation for my new home's front space.

Love your space. May these words and images inspire you to make your own home more curb appealing.

Michelle Valigursky

For years, my husband and I have loved taking long walks through neighborhoods to look at houses. When living in Maryland, we studied the stately traditionals of Bethesda and Chevy Case, and took sojourns into Georgetown and Old Town Alexandria to get lost among its tree-lined streets full of history. Once in New York City, our favorite pastime was to escape our one bedroom walk-up in Queens and take the train out to Brooklyn Heights and Park Slope. There we would imagine our dream life as *brownstoners,* a new term coined by Brooklyn resident and blogger Jonathon Butler to reflect city life in the Borough's upscale neighborhoods.

In Los Angeles, where each neighborhood had a different character, we never lacked for avenues to take time exploring. We loved Pasadena's Craftsman bungalows, Silverlake's blend of mid-century Moderns and 1930s Spanish, and Venice's artsy cottages, drawing inspiration from their eclectic appeal for our own home renovations. Now in our new hometown of Atlanta, we explore the in-town streets and historic industrial enclaves where Modern architects' homes sit side by side with quaint Depression-era cottages. We're forever fascinated by the creative expression of certain homeowners, the ones who understand dramatic curb appeal.

As a seasoned investor and home renovator, my passion for design sets my expectations high. I long to admire an arresting color scheme, or be tempted to follow a stone path leading to a seductive garden, or be inspired by an artistic use of materials and accessories. More often than not, however, most homes reflect "safe" choices in which exterior colors are bland, landscaping is ho-hum and building materials are ordinary.

My thoughts spring into action when I see a house longing for attention. I want to get my hands on it and make that home better! With just the right architectural accents and plantings, with a splash of color in a well-chosen location or a lighting scheme to highlight features, every home can boast outstanding curb appeal.

Everything you need to get started on your own exciting front-of-the-home transformation is right in your hands. Good luck. Most importantly, take some chances and have fun! I hope to be transfixed and delighted by your fabulous house on my next neighborhood exploration.

Lisa Vail

The escalating stone and slate chip path stops first at a front courtyard before continuing up to the front entrance of this hillside home.

Acknowledgments

The authors would like to thank the countless professionals and artisans who contributed their knowledge, expertise, time and enthusiasm to make this book such a special project. We appreciate that you so graciously allowed us to talk details with you and photograph your amazing work. In our travels, we would often happen upon and photograph an awe-inspiring home's front yard. These homes were eye-catching, well-designed, and epitomized the concepts we wanted to share with our readers.

Therefore, we wish to thank the unnamed architects, landscape designers, home builders, craftsmen, artisans, and homeowners whose front yards are extraordinary. Without the creative eye of Theresa M. Grant, our primary photographer, this book would not have been possible. We are also indebted to the staff at Schiffer Publishing for making our dream for the book a reality. Through the words and stunning photographs on the following pages, we hope to inspire you to create magnificent front yards of your own.

Chapter One
Planning a Balanced Space

A home's inspired front space takes on many definitions. No single architectural style, landscaping plan or fencing material can define it.

One characteristic, however, is common to all inspired front spaces: a well-planned design. Each element is carefully selected. Colors and architectural themes repeat. Additions and renovations are seamless, professionally done and respect the original structure. Landscaping befits not only the home's architecture, but also the regional terrain. From light fixtures and hardscaping to the chairs on the porch and the house numbers by the door – every detail is precise.

For example, the plum accent color on the windows of the house may be found again in the purple fountain grass that predominates the landscaping. Or, the gabled roof of a Craftsman home can recur in the arbor over the garden gate. Wrought iron fencing may again be reflected in lantern lights and house numbers. Complementary components such as these lend themselves to a balanced presentation.

You may be about to embark on a major overhaul of your property, complete with structural changes and large-scale hardscaping projects. Your improvement goals might focus on simple cosmetic changes such as new paint and plantings. Regardless of your project's complexity, your first step must be the same: *plan*.

We've all heard the phrase "two steps forward, three steps back." When you advance plan your front space project, you'll avoid this syndrome of making costly mistakes and reworking problems. After all, the best solutions evolve after hours of brainstorming, visualizing, researching and creative problem solving. Be patient. Allow your home to inspire you.

Pathways invite visitors to your home. Here, slate squares surrounded by smooth pebbles make a bold, visual statement. *Photo by Lisa Vail*

Opposite page:
Meandering stairs under a canopy of palm trees makes a grand entrance to this hilltop Spanish manse.

Quiet moments in a garden invite reflection and pause.

The Big Picture

To begin your front-of-home planning, assess what you have to work with. Unless you start from scratch with new construction, every home or site will have built-in and unchangeable parameters to be considered as you develop a big-picture plan for your home.

First things first: buy a notebook with pockets. Create sections for ideas, photographs, and plans. This book will quickly become an invaluable reference tool to organize notes, business cards, magazine clippings, snapshots, and sketches in one easy-to-access location.

With design notebook and pen in hand, walk across the street. Try to adopt the mindset of a first-time visitor as you preview your house and property. What is your overall impression? Record your observations.

Architect Miri Lerner emphasizes how important a well-defined entrance onto the property is to a first-time guest. "It is very disconcerting to be unsure how to approach someone's home -- quite the opposite of the welcoming message a visitor should be receiving." Analyze whether your entrance is well marked to ensure a guest's first experience of your home is positive.

While still out front, observe neighbors' homes, as well. Your house should reflect your style and personality, but your property is only a small facet of the neighborhood and should blend harmoniously with its surroundings.

Carry out this assessment until you've accounted for every element of your home's exterior. Repeat this observation process more than once, at different times of the day and in different weather conditions. The more you observe, the more familiar you will become with the characteristics that make your home unique.

Beginning with this in-depth property study serves a two-fold purpose. First, your written analysis will be a useful inventory and resource manual as you continue to plan. Second, you'll brim with ideas on how to make your home's front space more inspired. Carefully analyzing your home's presentation will jump-start your imagination into envisioning what it could become.

A stout row of conifers edge a lacy ironwork fence and rose-covered trellis in front of this Civil War-era home.
Photo by Nancy Fay

Placement of one rustic accessory
in a key location can complement a
home's tone and express personality.

The front porch exemplifies the perfect spot for
outdoor living. Homeowners convey their love of folk
art in this whimsical rooster painting.

Taking Stock

Author Michelle Valigursky follows the same process when she settles into each new family home. "Think of this as a getting-to-know-you exercise between you and your new house," she says. "Take your time and jot the answers to these questions in your journal as you evaluate your home in its present condition."

* When you look at your home from the curb, does it invite you in? Does it blend with the neighborhood yet display unique touches to personalize the property?
* What is your home's architectural style? Do any elements seem inconsistent? Are remodeling projects apparent in an unflattering way? Are architectural changes structurally sound and well-integrated?
* Is the exterior surface (wood siding, stucco, brick, etc.) original to the house? If not, is the material choice appropriate for your home? What is its condition?
* Study the home's color scheme. Is it aesthetically pleasing? Is the paint in good condition? Could you introduce additional accent colors?
* Is the path to the front door easily located both day and night? Is it wheelchair accessible? Do materials used complement the house? Is the pathway safe in all weather conditions, and in all types of shoes? Could the path layout be more visually interesting? Do you stray from the main path for a more convenient way to the front door? Do secondary paths follow the natural flow of foot traffic?
* What plantings thrive in your yard, as well as in your neighborhood and climate? Which plants look in ill health? Which plants do you love? Hate? How do changing seasons affect your landscaping? Does your current landscaping accentuate the house with a special aura, or is it dull?
* Is your property sloped or flat? Do hillside areas need retention or terracing? Could flat areas be converted to a patio or play area?
* If your garage is visible does it coordinate architecturally with the house? Could you customize the door by design or material

Trash cans do not have to clutter a front landscape. This cleverly constructed barrier serves as both a planter and a screen to hide bins.

choice? Is the driveway wide enough to support your family's parking and turnaround needs?
* Does your fencing or perimeter wall complement the style of your home? Does it need to be updated? Is it necessary at all?
* Is your exterior lighting both dramatic and effective? Can you add new lighting to spotlight a special planting, decorative object or architectural feature?
* Are your utility items such as a garden hose, trash can or gas meter hidden from view?

For a modern home, streamlined path design, lighting choices and planting schemes complement the design.

Making the Wish List

It's time to dream. That's right – you're about to create your fantasy wish list. Why? Capture your creativity when the ideas are bursting before tedious details like budgets and unchangeable site plans interfere with makeover decisions. Fantasize about your home's ideal front space. Grab your journal again and open to a fresh page.

What is the most fabulous house you can imagine? This may be a home you've visited or seen in a magazine. What features of this dream home speak to you? You're looking for elements of inspiration during this exercise – not a point-by-point match to your existing home.

Design psychologists Constance Forrest and Susan Lee Painter employ this exercise at the beginning of the design process. When Forrest and Painter sense a positive emotional connection to a home memory, they dig deeper to pinpoint specific details that can be introduced into their client's home life to renew these happy memories again and again.

Landscape designer Randy Anderson recalls one client's request to imbed her prized collection of shark's teeth into the paving material of her new front patio. Not only did they add a personal touch to the hardscaping, but they also evoked the secluded beach where she spent many peaceful hours combing for such treasures. Says Anderson: "It became my client's favorite part of the whole front yard landscape. She really enjoys pointing them out to new visitors and sharing how she found them."

During your project planning, seek inspiration wherever you can. Walk or drive through neighborhoods full of curb appeal, and take advantage of architectural and garden tours whenever they are available. Cut pictures from magazines and shoot digital photos of details that capture your attention.

When considering design of your home garden, take inspiration from your travels to botanical gardens and national parks. Like planners did in this temple garden in Asia, consider the way sunlight will linger on plantings and statuary. *Photo by Ed Valigursky*

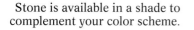
Stone is available in a shade to complement your color scheme.

Fountains can be custom made to depict a meaningful memory or allusion. At the Atlanta Botanical Gardens, artist Christine Sibley designed an 80-foot ceramic mural depicting water naiads, water lilies and lotus blossoms in bas relief.

Architectural salvage can add interest and dimension to your home's front space.

Even the smallest details hold meaning. Here, sharks' teeth embedded in a patio inspire thought-provoking memories for a homeowner. *Photo by Lisa Vail*

The ABCs of Design

Balance is accomplished through an equal distribution of "weight" in a design. Just as a chair must have the appropriate amount of legs to keep from tipping over, so must objects within a space to maintain visual stability. This can be achieved in one of two ways: symmetrically or asymmetrically. Symmetrical balance is the use of equal "weights" or objects on each side of a focal point. Identical potted plants to each side of a front door would be an example of symmetrical balance. If that same front door were flanked by a large potted plant to one side and three smaller (equaling the larger in visual weight) to the other, asymmetrical balance would be achieved.

Color evokes the most emotional, as well as physical, response in its viewer. It can create the feeling of warmth or coolness, relaxation or stimulation and can even raise a person's blood pressure! One's preference for colors sends messages as to whether one is friendly (orange), reserved (blue), or always on the lookout for a good time (red). Researchers can often pinpoint your age, gender, and economic status, just by observing your color choices.

Emphasis refers to the component in an arrangement that most captures a viewer's attention. There are various ways the principle of emphasis can be employed. Creating and designing around a focal point, repeating something you want to stand out and utilizing contrasts in color, texture, shape, and other elements to draw attention to a specific point are all effective tools to influence the observer's experience. You can also use these concepts to draw attention away from an unwanted focal point.

Form refers to an object with both shape and structure. It must be three dimensional (have height, width and depth) to differentiate it from a shape. For example, a triangle is a shape but a pyramid is a form. Cubes, spheres, pyramids, cones and cylinders are examples of various forms. In decorative elements, such as furniture, form is dictated by the purpose of the object. A chair, for instance, must have a horizontal plane for sitting to be defined as a chair.

Line refers to the continuous mark made on some surface by a moving point or, as artist Paul Klee once wrote, "A line is a dot that goes for a walk." It defines space, creates patterns and movement, and gives the illusion of mass or volume. Lines can have a psychological impact according to character and direction. Horizontal line (also known as *rectilinear*) suggests a feeling of repose, security, and masculinity. Soft, curving lines (or *curvilinear*) evoke feelings of comfort, familiarity and femininity. Line can move the eye through space, visually leading you to an intended focal point, such as a statue at the end of a path.

Pattern has a two-part definition: it is the repetition of shape, line, or color in a design as well as an underlying structure that acts as a skeleton for things both man-made and naturally-occurring. In Harvard biologist Peter S. Stevens' book *Patterns in Nature*, he claims patterns can be structured in only a finite number of ways and that grids are the foundation for all structures or images. Just scour your own home to find illustrations of nature's patterning, such as the spiral of a tulip and the branching of the trees. Roof shingles, clapboard siding

The repetition of curves in landscaping, lawn and driveway work in concert to create a graceful approach.

A unique way to add symmetry is through numerical positioning. Notice the four angels, three dwarf conifers, and two lamps over the prominent arched doorway.

and brick driveways show how material choices offer pattern to your home's exterior.

Proportion refers to the relationship between objects within a space and refers to the comparison of these objects in terms of size and scale. When something is "out of proportion," it has been determined it is either too large or too small in comparison to the most important object in that particular composition. For example, a picket fence would probably look disproportionately small in front of a stately manor house yet perfectly in proportion paired with a cozy cottage.

Rhythm refers to the visual and sensory reaction we experience in response to the recurrence of lines, shapes, forms or colors in a design. Just as we can feel and move to the repetitive beat of a drum, we also respond to the rhythms of our surroundings. The placement of stepping stones can have you literally skipping down a path; a spattering of red poppies can lead your eyes dancing through a planting bed. Rhythm depends largely on pattern to achieve its effects.

Shape is an enclosed space defined and determined by other elements such as line, color, value and texture. The two-dimensional character of shape distinguishes it from form, which has depth as well as length and width. Examples of shapes include: circles, triangles, squares and rectangles, as well as less-recognizable amorphous shapes. Generally speaking, a shape will either be geometric, natural, abstract or non-objective. Geometric shapes are often used in architecture, art, and are naturally occurring in nature, as well. Natural shapes are understood to include human, animal and plant shapes. Leaves, patterns on animals, and flowers are all examples. When a natural shape is distorted in such a way as to reduce it to its essence, we say it has been abstracted. Lastly, shapes that do not relate to anything in the natural world are termed non-objective.

Space refers to the distance or area between, around, above, below or within things. It can be two-dimensional or three-dimensional, positive or negative; and actual, illusionist and pictorial. Actual space is what designers and architects work with most. It is real space, both inside a structure and out. Positive and negative areas are also important aspects of space. Positive space in artwork or structure is filled with shapes, lines, color, etc. Negative space is the empty space around filled areas and is often as important as the positive.

Texture refers to the surface quality or "feel" of an object. Rough, warm, smooth, bumpy, hard, velvety -- these are possible textile sensations an object can elicit. Actual texture is something you can literally feel, like a stone wall. Visual texture gives you the idea of texture. Varying both actual and visual textures is an important concept to consider when designing, for doing so adds variety in what could otherwise be a very stagnate environment.

Unity and Variety go hand in hand. Unity encompasses the whole design, incorporating elements in a composition to achieve a harmonious result. Consistency is the key to unity. However, too much consistency can be boring and stagnate. A variety of elements that share the right mixture of commonalities (such as color, shape and texture) can achieve a well-balanced and pleasing space in an interesting and surprising way.

This contemporary home balances hard against soft, using rectilinear lines and repetition of shape to play off the texture of limestone block and the movement of grasses.

Research plants that thrive in your area and minimize need for water and maintenance. The rosette of this drought-tolerant echeveria exemplifies the natural spiraling that can occur in nature.

Dollars and Sense: Setting the Budget

Let's face it. Renovation involves far more than sweat equity alone. In most cases, change costs money. "When you start a project, whether you are a professional or a homeowner, budget must be up-front," according to Los Angeles Architect Jay Harik. "Your budget should drive your design concept and become your number one priority."

Be prepared to pare down your wish list. But don't get frustrated if financial resources are limited. Here's the critical point to remember: endless budget does not equate to great design.

Harik elaborates, "Your project does not have to suffer because you don't have deep pockets. When my client gives me a budget to work with, I see it as a challenge to come up with new, innovative ideas that might not have occurred to me if money had been no object. Some of my most exciting work has come out of such scenarios."

Atlanta Garden Designer Jenn Carr recommends developing a long-term, multi-phase plan for your exterior renovation. "My clients often choose projects to implement each season until they finally achieve their dream yard and garden. This enables them to make positive changes, over time, without breaking the bank. In the process, they gain tremendous satisfaction during each stage of the project."

It's time for a caveat regarding curb appeal. Patience is indeed a virtue to be admired. When people fall prey to the need for instant gratification, architectural integrity and common sense seem to fall by the wayside. Author Lisa Vail points out, "In Los Angeles, for instance, the character of historic homes is all too often destroyed by the application of stucco and generic vinyl windows as a way to bypass the regular maintenance and repair of wood siding and windows. Do the right thing. While tricks of the trade can stretch a design budget, some money-saving shortcuts are just not acceptable."

Left:
Many older homes featured carports, yet today's multi-tasking families need the security, storage and convenience of an enclosed garage. The re-purposing of a carport to enclosed garage gave much-needed space to this small ranch home.

Below, left:
An unexpected touch: a lion's head fountain graces a shady wall aside the front entrance of this refreshed Atlanta ranch.

Below, center:
Great design does not have to exceed budget. Clever use of paint applications and repetition of shape can maximize impact while minimizing expense.

Below, right:
Add dimension and humor to a space with a touch of hand-lettering.

Working with the Pros

When should you call in a professional?

If you can't wait to implement your own design, you'd fall into the category of the creative, do-it-yourself weekend warrior. Most likely you'll have the time, skill set and inclination to tackle many projects on your own. If that's the case, the tools, advice and inspiration on the following pages will guide you through the front-of-home transformation.

In later pages, we'll identify the tools you'll need to implement a specific curb appeal project. These may include how to use schematics and create hardscaping site plans. We'll also introduce you to high-tech solutions including specialized software and techniques for photographic manipulation.

But if the concept of single-handedly creating and overseeing every detail of your project seems out of your league, consider bringing on board one or more design professionals.

These experts, who will play key roles in the planning phase, may be landscape architects and designers, residential architects, contractors, and home designers. They specialize in renovation and share their knowledge, skill, and experience. Springboarding off your initial concept, they'll launch your project into a new realm of functionality, ingenuity, and aesthetics.

Professionals can assist by providing services such as site studies, structural or geological surveys, planning and zoning applications and code compliance. They will evaluate budget with recommendations for cost-saving materials and methods and monitor the progress and quality of workmanship in all project phases. Your professional will facilitate relationships with industry lighting and color specialists and coordinate contractor and service provider work schedules. Best of all, professionals can obtain materials available only to the trade.

Working through referrals is perhaps the best way to locate a professional. Leading experts in the field attain the majority of their clients this way. However, if you've recently relocated, you may also approach these organizations:

* The American Institute of Architects (AIA)
* The National Association of the Remodeling Industry (NARI)
* The Association of Professional Landscape Designers (APLD)

This garden unfolds in layers and levels, creating a complex and visually stimulating front space with striking color.

Roof gables and window shape echo to create balance in a home front.

Opposite page:
Perfect balance exists between the arched doorway, windows, path and shutter tops.

Begin your search by visiting association websites to identify members in your area. When considering candidates, always check references before making final decisions.

On the flip side, you may wait to be "chosen." Landscape Designer Judy Kameon, who generally has a six-month waiting list for her services, only takes projects that excite her. "I'm fortunate to stay busy and I often have to turn down job opportunities. For me to accept a new landscaping project, I must respond to the site, the architecture of the house and the client."

Architect Michael Hricak won't take a job he's not passionate about mainly because he feels someone else might be better suited. "I have a very modern aesthetic and I wouldn't feel comfortable working with someone who wanted a period-style renovation. We just wouldn't make a good match."

If you're on the receiving end of a "No, thanks," take it as a sign that the perfect partnership is still in the making. But once the match is made, get down to brass tacks and define the project scope in writing. A clearly defined contract with deadlines, deliverables and responsibilities will provide an essential roadmap for progress.

Trade Secret:

The best free source for detailed contract advice is the AIA website at www.ala.org. Though this focuses on the owner-architect relationship, these insights can be applied to any professional agreement. For more large-scale, complex projects, seek an attorney's counsel.

Thomas Jefferson proved more than 160 years ago that walls do not have to be built in straight lines when he created a serpentine wall for University of Virginia. Here, a sweeping curve creates an intimate dining nook on this patio. Notice the built-in drainage that acts as a design element. *Photo by Michelle Valigursky*

The Curb Appeal Perspective: Gut Reaction

A well-manicured front space shapes a buyer's impression of your home.

The French have a saying. It's *je ne sais quoi*. Literally translated, it means "I don't know what." They call upon the expression to describe something that delights the eye, something that possesses an intangible quality of beauty, grace or style that can't be compartmentalized into a simple descriptive.

In real estate, we might use the same phrase to define "curb appeal." Atlanta Real Estate Agent Sharon Cunningham explains.

"Curb appeal is not just about flowers or great trees. It's far more than exquisite lighting and windows. It even surpasses leaded glass doors or stonework or cobblestone paths. It's everything rolled into one complete presentation. To put it simply, curb appeal is WOW power."

As a homeowner, you must face economic reality. When your home is on the market, a sale is often made or broken based on a buyer's gut reaction when they set eyes on your home. Cunningham continues.

"Another benefit is purely monetary. Homes with manicured landscaping and well-maintained exteriors fetch higher sales prices and sell quicker than their counterparts that require far more sweat equity from new owners."

"Does your house have what it takes to pass that first crucial buyer test?" asks Alpharetta Real Estate Agent Pam Jeruss. "If the approach to your home is riddled with weeds, fallen tree limbs, a cracked driveway or mildewed siding, chances are the buyer will say 'Pass.' No matter how wonderful your home might be on the inside, that from-the-street first impression means everything. Fair or unfair, buyers often refuse to go inside a home based on its lack of curb appeal."

Real Estate Agent's Rule: People respond with every sense when they make home purchasing decisions. Attending to color, scent, texture, spatial arrangement and overall presentation from the curb to your front door will win over a buyer.

Dappled sunlight shimmers against stonework and sculpture to create mood lighting at varying times of day. *Photo by Michelle Valigursky*

Chapter Two
Architectural Solutions

Understanding your home's architectural style and history is the cornerstone of creating an awe-inspiring home front. Does your home reflect the linear progressions and sculptural forms of Le Corbusier? Does your brick-front colonial echo Jefferson's Monticello? Does your Craftsman pay homage to Greene and Greene's Gamble House? Knowing your home's architectural roots will help guide decisions when updates and additions are in order.

Pinpointing a home's specific architecture can be difficult, especially when so many homes feature a fusion of influences and details. Atlanta architect Lorraine Enwright elaborates: "Homes often begin with a historical reference to a style then incorporate fresh interpretations to make the design new." Within broad categories such as Cape Cod, ranch, Colonial, or Victorian, homes reflect a regional variation of visual features. These distinguishing architectural derivations can be attributed to the individual craftsmen who worked on the home's design and the families for which the homes were constructed. Today, as in the past, designers borrow elements from a variety of styles to create their own versions of the ideal home. Similarly, "revival" architecture, which nods back to particular historical periods, continues to be popular as builders adapt yesteryear's characteristics to fit modern-day needs.

Opposite page
Homeowners can mix elements from many eras of architectural design to achieve a front space with both historical reference and charm. This restored farm house has been refreshed with current paint colors and lighting, as well as new windows.

When designing front space, fencing and specimen trees can be integrated with future growth in mind.

If your home's façade is the victim of a *"remuddle,"* rescue its architectural integrity. New owners often inherit a past inhabitant's unsuccessful attempt to turn a house into something it can never comfortably be. A woodsy contemporary won't ever resemble a pseudo-historic English Tudor, no matter how many window boxes and brass coach lamps are inflicted upon it. Historic homes often undergo a series of changes, implemented over years by a succession of residents adapting the house to fit their own lifestyle and needs. A previous owner may have longed for a bigger living room so enclosed the front porch; another tired of maintaining the wood siding and covered it over with vinyl. One by one, ill-advised do-it-yourselfers contributed to the hodge-podge you're now in charge of fixing.

Your home's true character may not be tarnished forever just because previous owners have fulfilled their own tastes at the expense of aesthetics. Take the time to investigate your home's history and its original footprint may be revealed. Check for building permits in county records that might indicate how many bedrooms a home once had, or whether there was originally a front porch. Ask "old-timers" in the neighborhood to share their recollections of what once was and study the surrounding homes that look as if they were built by the same developer. Eventually, the pieces of the puzzle will come together, offering direction for your meticulous restoration or fresh interpretation.

Shutters and a pergola entry structure add dimension to this home's classic shape.

The garage is dressed up with a multi-window dormer and sections of galvanized roof panels.

Once Upon a Time

Before you move forward, you must first step back. After all, the history of your home and how it merges into the broader American landscape will inform each design decision in your inspired home transformation. In the earliest days of our country's history, buildings existed solely to provide shelter. New settlers arrived, bringing with them the construction techniques and design aesthetics of their homelands. By the early nineteenth century, an American style emerged through the brick row houses in Eastern cities and the wooden Greek Revival homes throughout the countryside made abundant with the circulation of popular pattern books.

The late 1800s introduced a new architectural style that rejected the foreboding Gothic style that preceded it. At this time, new middle class neighborhoods emerged on the edges of business and commercial districts, distinguished by fanciful Victorians and an intricate cable car system for downtown commutes. But since one building fad always gives way to another, gingerbread-laden trim work and fish-scale shingled Victorians were viewed as old-fashioned and pretentious by the early 20th century. The hot new import was England's Arts and Crafts Movement, which rejected superfluous, machine-made ornamentations and celebrated natural materials simply honed by skilled artisans. In what was by now an American tradition of borrowing and adapting architectural movements from other countries, Sears and Roebuck's borrowed the humble Craftsman concept and turned it into a multi-million dollar industry through its kit house catalog.

After World War II, suburbia flourished when G.I. mortgages and government incentives made home ownership more attainable. Rural areas outside of major cities were suddenly close in, thanks to the accessibility of the automobile and expanded highways. Perhaps the greatest influence on suburban development today was Levittown, built in the late 1940s and 1950s outside New York City. The quintessential "cookie cutter" planned community, Levittown offered affordable, detached single-family residences to G.I.s returning from World War II, as well as to families who wanted to move out of New York's boroughs into more spacious digs. For most residents, this was their first home purchase and an opportunity to achieve the American Dream (an ideal that Joseph Levitt himself propagated through clever marketing campaigns).

The variety of decorative detailing in the roof pattern, fish scale shingles, carved trim and turned balusters are characteristic of Victorian architecture.

Landscape Designer Judy Kameon took inspiration from the Neutra architecture when conceptualizing the design of this sculptural street-side landscaping.

On the other side of the post-war architectural fence, The Case Study House Program in Southern California challenged the idea that identical houses in planned developments were the only answer to U.S. housing needs. Among the eight architects involved in the program, begun in 1945, were legends Richard Neutra, Charles and Ray Eames, and Pierre Koenig. They designed groundbreaking ranch and cliff-side homes while experimenting with new materials and structural innovations. Many of our current housing trends, such as open floor plans, recessed lighting, and large expanses of glass that blur the division between outside and in are all byproducts of this era of ingenuity.

After the ranch craze swept the nation mid-century, architectural trends turned to the geometry and openness of 1970s contemporaries, the 1980s "four and a door" Colonials, and the 1990s mixed-material European imitations. Today, the ranches made famous during the mid-century period are again gaining in popularity.

Chimneys take on architectural interest when created from non-traditional materials. This stovepipe chimney complements the rustic home design.

Porch railings and materials depict unity with nature.

Pre-fabricated homes are not short on style; this modern construction home offers sleek style and top-quality construction.

The Green Scene: Kit Homes

Between 1908 and 1940, more than 75,000 Sears homes were built. Sears kit homes contained 30,000 pieces and cost between $600 and $6000. Though Sears may not be in the home-making business any longer, plenty of other manufacturers, both in the United States and abroad, continue to offer home-building kits that support passive solar design choices. Today, kits are available to make log homes, cabins, barns, domes and many other structures. Though designs may be basic, these kits are both cost and time-efficient with respect to planning and production.

Yankee Barn of New Hampshire, for example, offers post-and-beam homes. Their on-staff designers will consult with you to customize a design. Once an order is placed, the kit home is shipped and arrives on site ready to erect in a few weeks.

Modern homes, too, are pushing acceptance of "pre-fab" home construction with the highest quality standards and design aesthetics. Of note are Michelle Kaufmann's Glide-house™ and the modular Dwell Home. IKEA manufactures flat-pack BoKlok homes available to specialty builders for construction in pre-selected communities. Though not yet available in the United States, BoKlok, which translates to "Live Smart," is a new wave in affordable eco-housing that offers living around communal green spaces.

Architect Lorraine Enwright's traditional home gets a facelift with the addition of symmetrical gables, accent windows and fresh colors.

Renovate the Right Way

Imagine your unassuming rambler with dormers or a summer porch and you just might pinpoint the makeover direction that will let your home shine. The low profile, unpretentious simplicity, and rectilinear structure of the ranch's roof can springboard you into a retro, new modern, or Prairie style. Stucco-sided ranches can even go in the direction of adobe or Mission style. With so much of America's housing stock dating from the 1940s through the 1970s, renovation is all the rage.

"Renovation is a perfect solution for the client who appreciates many of the attributes of older homes, particularly the proximity to city centers and generous lots, but want to update them to accommodate modern needs and aesthetics," says Architect Lorraine Enwright, who specializes in transforming outdated split-levels and ranches with fresh new facades, interiors and additions. "The challenge of blending features may even lead to a different concept than originally conceived, which can be a wonderful result." Enwright's exterior renovations often include adding dormers, gables, porches,

Gutters are a necessary part of many roof styles. Here, contrasting paint and duplication of downspouts makes a design statement.

Garage doors mirror the architecture of the main home with multi-pane windows and decorative hardware. Structural supports are painted a complementary color to this home's roof and gutters.

revised door and window placement, and new siding material such as shingles and stacked stone to create a fresh take on traditional styling. Enclosing carports into garages with carriage-style gates completes the traditional transition.

More modern-minded homeowners and architects take the opposite approach to renovating their mid-century abodes, stripping away any traditional pretenses to reveal a sleek, rectilinear façade. Atlanta homeowners Jared and Laura England hired the modern architecture firm Plexus R+D to give their no-thrills 1959 bungalow more contemporary styling. The resulting design retained the original footprint but little else remains the same. The Englands added both commercial-grade aluminum windows and front door. They also replaced standard brick and vinyl siding with "steel cladding that gets its bright blue finish from a new architectural coating technology," says Jared. This cladding boasts a 50-year warranty, and repeats on the home's roof in a white finish. While other renovation choices were made with budget constraints, "This no-maintenance product was our big splurge." The Englands, like other homeowners with wish lists, conceived plans that required modifications to suit the site and the scale of other homes in the neighborhood.

In-town neighborhoods across the country are also seeing radical changes to their community's landscape as many homebuyers opt to tear down and build anew instead of renovating or adding on. "People buy perfectly functional older homes at a premium where land is scarce but location is great," Enwright contends. "The mid-century home doesn't always adapt well. Low ceilings, small rooms, and disjointed interior traffic flow may make renovation difficult. In these cases, the only cost-efficient solution to attaining the lifestyle the customer wants is to tear down and start fresh."

Massachusetts Architect David Sharff faces a different challenge, that of adapting historic houses to accommodate 21st century families. "These are gorgeous homes but we simply have different lifestyle needs today. Past homeowners had a separate room for every function, from front parlors to maid's quarters, and kitchens were tiny and tucked out of sight.

An inside look at the portico. In this small space, angles and depth turn an ordinary beadboard ceiling into a work of art.

An arched window in the portico over the front door and sidelites offers filtered sunlight in the home's side entrance addition.

The pendulum has now swung towards multi-purpose great rooms that open onto expansive gourmet kitchens." Another top renovation request? More space.

Sharff acknowledges that many of his home additions are built onto the side of a house, which alters the front façade. This can be tricky when the new construction must be perfectly reconciled with the original structure. This is where Sharff's extensive knowledge of period architecture and historical preservation come in handy. "The transition from old to new should be seamless. I know I've achieved my goals when an addition looks like it's always been there." He best accomplishes this by carefully matching architectural features and siding materials, though less conservative clients may take this opportunity to replace an undesired material for something new. The most popular choice in his area is weathered shingles for its New England classicism. His final thoughts on renovating an old house the right way: "Respect for the original home is key to a successful renovation."

Hiring an Architect for Your Home's Exterior Facelift: The Process Revealed

To demystify the process of working with an expert, Atlanta Architect Lorraine Enwright recommends:

* *Create a program.* This design industry term equates to a wish list. Compile a notebook of magazine clippings, material samples and other articles of inspiration that can be shared with the design professionals who will implement your home's transformation.

* *Choose an architect whose work speaks to you.* Evaluate finished projects and ask for specific referrals from existing and past clients. Make sure you and your architect agree on issues of style and substance.

* *Meet in person at your home.* Because this will be a long-term relationship, be sure your personalities can coexist on a daily basis. You want to have the meeting on site, so the architect can understand the existing features and the scope of the project.

* *Determine how the architect will be paid.* Most architects work on a percentage basis depending on the complexity of the project: 6 to 8 percent of total construction cost for a small project, 10 to 15 percent for a midsize project, and 15 to 20 percent for a full-scale project. Or, for simple consultations, architects will often work on an hourly rate of $80 to $200 an hour, depending on expertise.

* *Review conceptual studies.* The architect will produce conceptual studies based on your program that will allow you to explore multiple design options. Be open-minded to your architect's unexpected suggestions; after all, you're paying for their creativity and expertise!

* *Meet with the architect to select a plan.* With solutions in hand, the architect will meet with you to discuss the chosen plans. Now is the time to ask for any last minute changes; once in the construction phase, changes will be costly.

* *Get estimates.* When a final design is selected, the architect will obtain a rough price from general contractors. Choosing the right building team is as crucial as your choice of architect and merits the same due diligence. Remember: the cheapest price is not always the wisest deciding factor.

* *Approve budget and final plans.* When you have approved plans and budget, the necessary permits will be obtained by the general contractor. Schedules will be coordinated to select materials and arrange work calendars. This process may also include coordination of efforts by landscape architects who lay out hardscaping and planting beds.

Architect Lorraine Enwright believes that home renovations should begin with a historical reference then use fresh interpretations to make it personal. Here, she's incorporated banks of architectural windows, timbering, gables and arches to give this split-level ranch an extraordinary makeover.

* *The architect will supervise the project.* The general contractor will be your day-to-day onsite contact during the renovation, but the architect will stay actively involved to oversee progress and resolve unforeseen issues.

* *Once construction is complete, the architect will conduct the final walk-through with you to ensure code compliance and finished quality of workmanship.* A checklist of unfinished details, known as a punch list, will be created if needed. Speak up if you find anything unsatisfactory, and be sure to withhold final payment until the project is truly complete.

The Stucco Chronicles

Nothing stirs more controversy than the application of stucco. When applied correctly, hard coat stucco is versatile, an excellent energy-efficient insulator, and the perfect complement to certain architectural styles. But trouble looms when hard-coat or synthetic stucco are applied to a home erroneously, whether it's that the application itself is poor or simply that a stucco exterior does not suit the home's design.

Sadly, the character of an entire neighborhood can be lost to an epidemic of bad design decisions. Members of Los Angeles' numerous historical societies watch in horror as wood shingles and clapboard are ripped off turn-of-the-century bungalows in preparation for new stucco exteriors. These banal attempts at modernization only result in a featureless uniformity that lacks the charm and detail of the original structures.

If you've inherited a Craftsman, cottage, or Victorian home that has fallen prey to a hasty application of stucco, check to see if the original siding has been preserved beneath the stucco, chicken wire, and tarpaper. David Zanhiser of the Echo Park Historical Society teaches de-stucco workshops and says it's relatively easy to remove the unwanted layers with a hammer, a crowbar, and a pair of wire cutters. For more details on removing stucco, visit the Echo Park Historical Society website at www. historicechopark.org. Note that historic houses aren't the only residences plagued with stucco concerns. In the Southeast, stucco is being removed from homes built in the last 20 years because of improper application and maintenance. "Stucco is never the problem—it's a terrific insulator and it offers greater design flexibility than other building materials," says Bob Lemoine, owner of The Residential Inspector of America home inspection company. "But years of improper application have resulted in significant underlying moisture and mold issues for homeowners."

Lemoine explains. "With the older barrier systems, homes were designed with no way for moisture to weep out, which encouraged mold growth and termite infiltration, which in turn led to structural damage. Now, homes must have a proper drainage system and no earth-to-stucco contact to prevent access by termites."

So what can homeowners do to determine whether their homes suffer from stucco moisture damage? Lemoine recommends the following:

* Select a qualified stucco inspector who is EDI (Exterior Design Institute) certified, ASHI (American Society of Home Inspectors) certified, or local building code certified. Have the home moisture tested.
* Have the inspector determine the need for flashing, caulking, bottom-edge termination, and other essential repairs.
* Have the inspector recommend repairs for cracks, bulging, and holes.
* Consider purchasing a moisture-free warranty.

Jeff Shea of The Siding Doctor, a home improvement company specializing in exterior finishes, is often called in to remove stucco and replace it with HardiePlank™ fiber cement siding. "In nearly every case, the window seals and the roof flashing are deficient," Shea explains. "The mitre joints are critical, and the sad fact we discover is that most of these aren't even caulked. Window screens, too, can perpetrate problems. When water blows in through the screening, it often gets trapped and can seep into any open joints."

Shea points out, "We often remove stucco to reveal thousands of dollars in underlying wood rot and other structural damage. This all must be repaired before any reconstruction can begin." As with many aspects of home construction and renovation, the source of problems can often be traced back to the application rather than the product. Choose a contractor with certification in the material you wish to have installed to minimize the risk of costly repairs down the line.

Homeowners mark their home's entry with stuccoed pillars and a sturdy but decorative gate in this California home. This house was designed by Frank Lloyd Wright's son Lloyd Wright, who went on to be a renowned architect. Notice the very "Wrightian" (as in the elder Wright) design in the gate.

Often associated with Spanish style homes, stucco can be tinted in many shades to reflect the colors of nature.

Material Choices Abound

Historic preservation aside, some architects believe regional climate should influence exterior architectural finishes. Architect Michael Hricak agrees with selecting environmentally appropriate materials. "A clapboard or shingle house in New England can last three hundred years with normal maintenance because the climate is always moisture-laden, in hot or cold," he explains. "In Los Angeles, the weather is extreme. The wood completely dries out then gets wet again, then dries again, etc. The wear-and-tear cycle of drying and moisture absorption causes the wood to warp."

He proposes an innovative solution. "We shouldn't be using wood in Southern California. Instead, we need to develop a culture of building in light-weight steel, which addresses some of these issues. Texas limestone is another cutting edge solution." Change may come slowly, he admits. "Unfortunately, you can't beat the price of wood."

Professionals rely on a number of commonly used materials:

* **Brick:** A natural cladding material comprised of clay and water that has been fired in a kiln until hardened. This material dates back to ancient Mesopotamia, where it came into use around 500 B.C., and is available in various colors determined by the region of the clay. Resists pests and fire, insulates naturally. Highly durable.

* **Fiber cement:** A combination of Portland cement, sand, and wood fibers. Also known as cement fiberboard, it comes in a variety of finishes and shapes, including shingle and clapboard styles stamped to emulate real wood and smooth or stucco panels for a contemporary look. A low maintenance, high endurance product material, available in a plethora of pre-painted fade-resistant colors. The innovator of this technology is the James Hardie company; the term HardiePlank™ has become synonymous with fiber cement siding.

* **Stone:** Veneers of river rock, flagstone, and slate. A popular choice is Austin stone (named for the stone quarries of Austin, Texas). Stone is also now available in man-made varieties using Portland cement, natural aggregates, and raw oxide pigments. New materials also provide the look of an architectural stone finish using interlocking pre-cast concrete tiles, eliminating the need for mortar and its associated problems.

* **Stucco:** A material mixed from cement, water, and sand, common in Mission, Mediterranean, and Italianate homes. Stucco is applied over a lath framework that has first been covered by tarpaper and chicken wire.

* **Wood siding:** Can be beveled, lap, or board and batten design. Cedar is the most commonly used wood siding because of its strength, durability, and natural resistance to moisture and insect damage. Wood siding may be painted or stained; staining retains an attractive grain.

When designed well, a combination of exterior finishes can add visual texture and interest to a home's façade. Now that the builder's favorite combo of brick, stacked stone and shingle has become ubiquitous across the country, more creative mergers provide a refreshing change of scenery. Trend-setting architects pair simple materials such as concrete block, reinforced concrete panels, and smooth stucco finishes with eye-catching accents in plywood, galvanized metal, copper sheathing and stained exotic woods. A change in material works best when it coincides with a different plane, as when an addition has been offset from the original structure or a protruding architectural element such as a gable, pediment or front porch is highlighted. Unless you are rehabbing a Victorian (in which a medley of siding finishes, shapes and colors was typical), it's best to limit the number of siding materials to avoid a "busy" appearance.

Architect Lorraine Enwright's renovations often mix Old World materials like stacked stone, brick and shingle with creative contemporary details like this band of fun windows.

Renovations of traditional residences take on new dimension when materials are mixed, as done here by Architect David Jameson in this suburban Maryland stone and concrete design.

Quaint cottages don't have to mean constant maintenance. Here, HardiePlank™ keeps the home virtually maintenance free. *Photo by HardiePlank™*

Architect Scott West built a modern masterpiece on a small mid-town Atlanta lot, designing his home with vertical lines in complementary planes of color and material. Materials vary from plane to plane to highlight the home's dimensions. The front courtyard is ipe wood. *Photo by Scott West*

Overhead

"When selecting a new roof, evaluate the total image you'd like your home to project, and consider standards set by homes in your neighborhood," says Glenn Mobley, President of J&M Roofing. "Your roof will become a focal point for your home and may be one of your largest investments." Mobley advises clients to understand regional climate before making material and ventilation choices. "While soffit, exhaust, turbine, static, and gable vents may provide adequate ventilation on their own, a combination method will produce the best results. In areas of high heat, consider using energy-efficient ridge vents. These will alleviate attic heat and moisture build-up which can lead to premature decay of shingles." Similarly, extreme cold requires roofing ventilation consideration to prevent ice dams and water vapor issues.

Depending on your home's intended design aesthetic, clay tiles, slate shingles or an architectural fiberglass asphalt shingle may best accomplish your goal. For Spanish, Southwestern and Italianate residences, roofing manufacturers now produce lighter-weight fiber cement versions that mimic classic clay tiles. These imitations are often made using recycled wood fiber and waste paper.

"High-end roofing products are thicker and more durable than ever before. Many offer material warranties for as long as 60 years, which helps to justify the higher initial investment," Mobley says. In the Atlanta suburbs he services, "Most homeowners are design-savvy and want to make an architectural statement with their roofs, rather than purchase the least expensive three-tab shingle option." He points out that the latest roofing technology includes products designed to resist mildew, fading, and wind and hail damage. Another upside to asphalt shingles, besides being budget friendly, is a wide range of colors.

Metal roofs, typically manufactured from fire-resistant aluminum, steel or copper, can expand and contract in response to temperature changes. Often made with recycled post-consumer waste, a variety of factory-applied paint finishes are available and include silicone and resin-based treatments that carry up to 20-year warranties. A

The multi-faceted colors of the architectural roofing are reflected in the brick-work and soft teal trim. *Photo by Nancy Fay*

common configuration for these eco-friendly roofs is the sleek standing-seam application.

A change in the roof's contours and pitch will make an even more dramatic transformation to a home's front view. Architect David Sharff recalls a split-level ranch renovation in which a new roofline design was the key component to its updated yet classic new exterior. The design objective for this home was two-fold: add more livable space as well as project a look more in keeping with New England's regional architecture. Says Sharff, "By adding a second story and redesigning the roof's pitch and profile, we were able to trick the

Research roofing appropriate to your home's style. On this farmhouse, galvanized roofing is aesthetically pleasing and long-lasting.

eye into seeing a more traditional house." A less expensive way to project an old-world influence is to add well-placed and proportioned dormers and gables. Besides being a hallmark characteristic of Early American architectural styles, dormers add dimension to the roofline and allow more light to penetrate interior spaces.

Soffits like these wood panels can reinforce a home's design.

Architectural vents near the roofline draw the eye up to an unexpected detail.

Rather than settle for a simple ceiling, this columned porch showcases this Japanese-inspired home's use of deep-toned wood.

The Curb Appeal Perspective: Look For Needy Homes

Spanish Colonial Revival architecture offers unique sculptural possibilities, such as this striking towering turret.

It's time for some training in spotting latent curb appeal. When you drive by that lavender home with the yellow and chartreuse trim, do you see anything but the color? Do you notice the sweep of roofline or the gentle shade created beneath the front porch? Are you able to look beyond the tacked-on addition or clumsy alteration to imagine how grand this home once was and could be again?

"You've got to train your eye to see potential," says Deana Vinovich, a real estate agent in Illinois. "Many homes suffer in the aftermath of incredibly poor design decisions. But once they're scrubbed clean, an investor can make real profit by showcasing the architecture."

Necessary changes might be simple or complex. For example, older split level homes might look sensational with bigger windows, traditional shingle siding, and the addition of a front porch. A too-flat Cape Cod might benefit from gabled dormers. The drab Colonial might become a gem with a columned portico and bay window. However, Austin Real Estate Agent Kelly Thate voices a concern about major changes: "Renovations without an architect are an absolute no-no. Architects ensure great flow in a home."

Be on the lookout for ways to add square footage to living space at minimal cost, since this is one of the best ways to add instant value to your real estate. Westcott Development's founder Ed Smith reclaimed a nondescript front porch on a 70s-era Colonial in Atlanta. "The tile flooring was badly in need of renovation, so we replaced it with natural stone. When we installed wrought iron railings to define the space, we created a perfect outdoor living room."

Connecticut Real Estate Broker Terry Keegan added a garage to his own historic home where none had ever existed. "Older homes can be quite small. Our architect made sure that the garage building complemented the design seamlessly and the added space has boosted our property value tremendously."

Don't be blinded by ugly paint, scrubby yards and uninformed architectural alterations that can be easily remedied. Evaluate the bones before rejecting a home's potential. Plenty of would-be buyers turn down the diamonds in the rough that savvy investors snatch up below market value and resell at huge profits. But like a successful professional rehabber, you must not only be able to recognize latent potential but know how much it will cost to exploit it.

Los Angeles Real Estate Broker and investor Michael Caldwell has witnessed too often the disastrous results of amateur flips. "Reality shows about flipping houses have made everyone want to get in on the game, hoping to make a quick buck. But without real know-how about what things cost and how much time the process will take, investors can easily find themselves in over their heads and out of money to finish the job or pay their mortgage." Caldwell also cautions against over-improving for the neighborhood, a trap both investors and homeowners renovating for their own needs fall prey to. "Area comps will impose a cap on how much your home can sell and appraise for, regardless of how appealing a renovation may be."

Real Estate Agent's Rule: The secret to finding a hidden real estate gem is identifying architectural promise and knowing how to cultivate it to reap huge financial rewards.

Opposite page: The addition of all-weather drapery panels creates an outdoor living space that can be enjoyed throughout the seasons and adds value to potential homebuyers.

Chapter Three
Front Yard Living

When Jane Jacobs' *The Death and Life of Great American Cities* was published in 1961, neighborhoods were changing, and not necessarily for the better. City-dwellers fled to the rapidly developing suburbs in droves, lured by the promise of a better life. To most, this meant a big lawn in front of a big house and an even bigger private backyard to which they would retreat. Jacobs lamented the loss of "the eyes on the street," that constant presence of pedestrians and porch-sitters that kept neighborhoods vital and crime down.

But now, New Urbanist planners and builders are bringing the concept of community back in vogue. New developments feature homes with front porches, close to the street and each other, and sidewalks lead to parks and businesses. Our streets and front yards are seeing a renaissance of activity at long last.

You don't have to live in Seaside, Florida; Serenbe, Georgia; or Kentlands, Maryland to reclaim your front yard as viable living space. After all, entertaining, gardening, playing with the kids or unwinding after work doesn't have to be relegated to the backyard, especially if yours doesn't offer conditions suitable to these activities.

As Landscape Designer Judy Kameon points out, "Most people think of their front yard as transitional space to be passed through, and not as a place for spending time on a regular basis. However, I have had clients with little or no backyard and limited space indoors, but lots of room out front. In these cases, it just made good sense to take advantage of that unused space."

When you think outside the box of your back yard, courtyards, terraces and front porches are obvious settings from which to experience the front of your home, but even a pair of Adirondack chairs strategically placed can capture a special view, or a small bench to the side of your entryway can become a welcomed waiting spot.

A fanciful Victorian-style lawn chair gives Master Gardener Ellen Ungaschick a place to enjoy her handiwork.

In the curving sweep of a front yard's well-defined boundary, this bench offers spectators a perfect view of lawn activities.

Opposite page:
Reviving a sense of community, many families choose to gather on front porches and patios to share time with neighbors and friends.

A Little History

In *The American Porch*, Michael Dolan traces the porch back to prehistoric times, where man watched the world from cave entrances. He says, "Here, in a zone that linked the privacy of the cave to the public realm of forest and field, the first tendrils of community wove themselves into the human nervous system." Throughout history, Dolan contends, "Every social stratum had its version of the porch – even poor city-dwellers had their stoop, where inevitable social interaction was the intention for sitting there."

Architect Michael Hricak and Design Psychologist Susan Lee Painter agree. Whereas back yards promote solitude, both think of the front yard as the "edge," the in-between zone of public and private space, and the place where we can feel connected to our neighborhood.

This inviting front space shines with color and personality.

In Victorian times, socializing was an out-front activity. Back yards were meant for utility and storage, harboring the outhouse, coal heaps, work sheds and carriage house. As industrialization modernized our home lives with indoor plumbing, electricity and central heat, people drifted their socialization toward the back of the house. By mid-century, perception had shifted and homeowners shied away from lingering on the "old-fashioned" front porch and preferred the privacy of the back yard space. Back patios were in, soon to be followed by decks.

Homeowners enjoy even the warmest summer evenings on this Victorian's front porch, thanks to a ceiling fan.

Create an Outdoor Room

Take an existing house, add a handful of building materials and a whole lot of physical labor and you might wind up with a great looking porch – or not. In Architect David Sharff 's Massachusetts-based business, a front porch or entrance is a top five request from clients contemplating renovation. "Here in New England it's critical. Just yesterday as it poured cold rain, I waited for the school bus with my daughters on our front porch."

Sharff explains, "I take advantage of the design of a front porch to reinforce the architecture of a house." He points out that individual architects will take a different approach to the same project. "Even when working on a home built to a specific style, like Greek Revival, it's important to remember houses are all different. Much depended on who built the home or the desire of the clients who commissioned the work. So, who's to say a curved porch couldn't have been built instead of a linear one?"

Porches give your home architectural presence and make ideal outdoor rooms. They can be screened to provide protection from pesky mosquitoes and could even be fitted with storm windows for year round use. Shelter beneath its eaves lets you enjoy a summer rain and allows you to choose from a wider selection of furniture and fabrics when making decorating decisions.

Most people think of a patio as a backyard staple, but it's also a great way to lend permanence to an outdoor front

The graceful curves of the shade porch round out the lines of this Greek Revival home.

A small front porch is extended by a stone patio to greatly expand outdoor living space. *Photo by Nancy Fay*

space. Author Michelle Valigursky suggests enclosing a patio and transforming it into a courtyard. "Add French doors or a folded glass wall to the living room and you've got spillover space for parties. Pave a pleasant spot amongst your landscaping to become a garden room. Your out-front patio doesn't have to be a boring concrete slab," she says. "Build one from a pea gravel bed, organically-shaped flagstone, or intricate brick patterns. If the patio is contiguous to the house, you need to consider both interior and exterior flooring. Think of sun, scenery and breeze. Do you need easy kitchen access? Good light for reading? Adequate entertaining space?"

Container gardens add punch to a simple front porch while the pair of Adirondack chairs offer a quiet place to enjoy the outdoors.

When yard space is fully landscaped, a high porch offers a bird's eye view of gardens.

Don't forget about roof space when designing outdoor rooms. In this modern home, each outdoor space offers a unique vantage point of the property and surrounds.

A home's placement on a site can influence use of outdoor space. This modern home was positioned in such a way that homeowners could enjoy full views of an adjacent lake from their full-length deck.

To take advantage of a beautiful garden and yard, Landscape Architect Graham Pittman created a secluded patio for dining al fresco.

Mixed materials offer contrast and texture in outdoor rooms.

Sections of latticework and an arched garden entry offer an intriguing destination for the family to explore.

Can We Get Some Privacy?

A fenced courtyard garden uses shade-loving grasses, creeping jenny and hosta plants to soften a patio. *Photo by Michelle Valigursky*

An extensive front yard patio surrounded by sculpted trees and plants provides the perfect setting for parties and relaxation. *Photo by Michelle Valigursky*

Frances Hodgson Burnett stirred a passion within us all when she wrote *The Secret Garden*. Children daydream of private breezy playrooms with canopies of leaves overhead and crunchy twigs beneath their feet. Adults long for secluded areas shaded by fragrant blooms. While the backyard seems like the perfect location for such a private hideaway, space or site restrictions might limit possibilities.

Author Michelle Valigursky created a private garden in a front space just below street level. "We'd occasionally walk the dog on a deer path through the woods. Down a gentle slope, the area was shielded from the street. After adding rock ledges and a thick mulch pathway and bench, I created a dry rock waterfall to maneuver natural runoff. Enjoying this hideaway planted with ferns and colorful shade blooms has become a daily ritual."

So what is the best way to plan a private garden room? Keep it low-key and small to retain coziness, just large enough for a café table and chairs or chaise lounge. Choose a location away from noise and traffic, when possible. Otherwise, use screening and a fountain to keep out the busy world. If not connected to the house, build a simple path leading to your garden room with pine bark or pebbles. And to retain privacy year round, use evergreen shrubs or hedges.

Landscape Designer Judy Kameon has also designed private spaces for the front of her clients' homes. "In some front yards we hedge or wall in all or a portion of the space, creating a courtyard. In a sense, the front yard then becomes the first room of the house. A visitor is treated to a layered experience."

Courtyards are characteristic of the Spanish Colonial and Mediterranean style homes found throughout California and other Southwest regions.

The main and secondary front paths converge as they lead to a pergola-covered, flagstone patio. Since this home has very little backyard, Landscape Designer Randy Anderson created a prominent outdoor living space that proudly dominates the front landscape. *Photo by Lisa Vail*

With the formality and symmetry of an English garden, this delightful front yard patio doubles as the front entrance and gives sophistication to this otherwise conventional suburban home.

A full-height door leading into a courtyard signifies that you are entering the first "room" of the house.

But other types can benefit from the courtyard concept, as well. The key is to forgo stucco walls and terracotta pavers for materials more complementary to your home's style. Kameon discusses the versatility of materials she's used to achieve non-traditional courtyard spaces. "We've done projects with custom-steel and frosted glass screens, hedging, mixed shrubs, walls and fencing. There are many different ways to create private outdoor rooms to complement personal and architectural style, but appropriate material choices are essential to success."

Even shady zones can reveal pools of filtered sunlight perfect for a bistro set or lounge chair for sunbathing.

The Decorator's Touch: Fabric and Furniture

Top decorators understand the value in carrying this same attention to detail to the outdoor spaces. "People should enjoy all facets of their homes," says Amy Novek, an interior designer in New Jersey. "Fabric and furniture manufacturers have addressed our need to expand our living space to the outdoors. While once we only had a handful of selections for weatherproof fabric, now we have hundreds of choices in pattern, texture and weight. It's a fabulous way to express personal taste."

Novek recommends evaluating the exterior space to be decorated by asking three important questions. How much sun exposure will the space get? Will fabric and furniture be regularly protected from the elements? If not, are you willing to remove or cover cushions and furniture during inclement weather and the off-season?

The answers to these questions will determine how durable your outdoor furniture will need to be. Wicker chairs with lovely cotton fabric cushions should need little upkeep on the front porch, but not everyone is up to the task of bringing them in from the uncovered patio every time the sky looks threatening. Consider opting for low-maintenance materials like aluminum and Sunbrella® fabrics.

Avoid the temptation to buy your furniture in "suites" or have everything covered in the same fabric. Says Novek, "Mix and match your fabrics. Choose complementary shades in a burly textured fabric to provide visual interest to a seating arrangement.

On a porch or beneath an arbor where sun and rain exposure will be limited, experiment with a palette of patterned and solid cotton blends for cushions, throw pillows and tablecloths." Author Lisa Vail adds, "I pair unique finds, like the pair of bamboo folding chairs I discovered at an import store, with other pieces I have collected in my travels. I use my knowledge of scale, line, color and shape to determine if an arrangement works, rather than obeying outdated rules about what 'goes together.'"

When it comes to furniture style, Outdoor Designer Robin Nowicki advises her clients to choose classics. "Because furniture is an investment, I want my clients to enjoy their choice for many years. My favorite is molded cast iron with a bronzed finish. It's fairly ornate, holds up to all types of weather and needs very little maintenance. For the Northeast it's perfect – you don't have to bring it in during winter."

Another great option in warmer climates is synthetic all-weather rattan, as opposed to the natural variety, and the modern offerings of plastic, aluminum, stainless or powder-coated steel. Two newcomers to the outdoor furniture arena are ipe (pronounced ee-pay) and nyatoh, non-endangered hardwoods prized for durability, strength, price and good looks.

For a more artistic approach to furnishing outdoor spaces, look beyond tradition. Tree seats, hand chiseled stone benches and hammocks provide privacy, seating and relaxation with a flash of personality.

Designer and mosaic artist Jo Beserra has decorated his front patio with as much attention to comfort and personal expression as the interior of his home. *Photo by Jo Beserra*

Even a narrow porch or patio can
accommodate a chaise lounge.
Photo by Michelle Valigursky

Artwork isn't just for indoors. Here, a fun painting graces a porch
with a bold punch of color.

The porch swing gets an update with
galvanized chains and fresh color.

The Curb Appeal Perspective:
Don't Waste Space

Atlanta Real Estate Agent Laura Law has witnessed clients fall in love with a home as soon as they see its gracious front porch. "In the South, we tend to live outside year round. Porches are a way of life. The grand old homes of the in-town neighborhoods here in Atlanta often have porches with swings and fans on their beadboard ceilings," she explains. "When a porch is done right, with comfy furniture and potted plants, clients know they'll want to spend time there, enjoying their neighbors' company and relaxing after a long day's work. A great porch can be a tremendous asset to a home."

To the contrary, a poorly maintained porch can signal disaster from a buyer's perspective. "If paint is peeling on the steps and the floorboards creak before you ever get to the front door, the client's mind is already made up. This isn't a home they'll want to live in because too much needs to be done," says Colleen Geppi, a Maryland real estate agent. "It's a first impression the home seller won't be able to change. And that's an opportunity lost."

Remember the real estate agent's motto: people buy square footage. Create outdoor rooms to increase your home's square footage. If you live in an area perfect for young families, add value to your home with a "child-watching" area.

"As every mom with toddlers knows, a good part of every day is spent supervising little ones riding bikes or playing ball on or near the driveway," Geppi explains. "The savvy homeowner will lend permanence to this activity and carve out a comfortable nook for adults. Add a half-moon patio with a wrought iron set or comfy teak chairs and an umbrella table. Buyers appreciate the forethought."

Landscape Designer Judy Kameon says, "Many clients request front yard living spaces. With some sort of enclosure around this area, as in a courtyard, parents can feel safe to let their children play out front."

Real Estate Agent's Rule: Don't waste space in your yard. Create reading nooks, exercise zones, gardening spots and play areas to expand your home's square footage potential.

Kids' playthings find a comfortable home at the edge of a shady drive.

Waiting for the bus is more pleasant in the garden's lacy ironwork seat beneath a shade tree.

A vintage tree bench adds a hint of old-fashioned charm. *Photo by Michelle Valigursky*

Chapter Four
Living With Color

Color means impact. And on your home's exterior, no single element can change perception, alter mood or add drama more effectively than its color scheme.

Cerulean blue. Mango cream. Mother of pearl. Whisper pink. The names alone trigger emotions, but the colors themselves often evoke a reaction far more physical. As Artist Wassily Kandinsky said, "Color acts upon the human body; it is the key touched by man to obtain the appropriate vibration from his creative spirit."

Colorwashing allows an infusion of hue without the saturation of a full-strength paint application and adds instant age to Italianate and Spanish-style architecture.
Photo by Lisa Vail

Opposite page:
Consider the hues of the natural landscape and the sun before selecting a final home color. This bold yellow can withstand the bright California sunshine.

Fencing and gates do not have to be white. Here, richer hues echo the tones of the florals and greenery to frame the garden with color. Accent tiles add an additional burst of color.

Consider the shade of your stonework when selecting contrasting, vibrant florals.

Design Psychologists Constance Forrest and Susan Lee Painter, who explore the critical role our surroundings have on our emotions, believe color has a stronger impact on our well-being than most of us realize. As both clinical psychologists and professional interior designers, they have done extensive research into the psychological and neurological origins of what they call "the yes response," that positive intuitive reaction we have to certain colors and objects.

When working with their clients to make color decisions, their goal is to implement these emotional triggers into their design as often as possible. In addition to a lengthy interview process that explores their client's life experiences with color, they'll sometimes use a thematic photograph or image the client responds to, then extract a color palette from that image.

Color Specialist Barbara Jacobs employs a similar approach. She points out, "Beyond creating beautiful and harmonious spaces, color has a profound impact on our psychological and physiological conditions. I love helping people discover the colors and combinations of colors that elicit that feeling of "AHA!" in them."

With evidence supporting the impact color has on our happiness, it's amazing how few homeowners use it to their advantage. The overabundance of ho-hum exterior color schemes suggests a widespread fear of making color decisions. That's perfectly understandable; after all, combining colors in a pleasing way takes patience and knowledge. But with rewards so great - to be delighted by colors you love that complement your home so befittingly — the time and effort it takes to get it right is well worth it.

Hiring a Color Specialist

Color specialists can provide a new way of looking at how colors can enhance a building and introduce you to creative color schemes you might never have imagined on your own. To make the process educational and participatory, Barbara Jacobs suggests:

* Decide on the scope and budget for your project.
* Drive through your neighborhood and note color palettes that speak to you.
* Gather photographs, swatches and other colorful sources of inspiration.
* Determine if historical accuracy is a priority.
* Be patient with the process. Color design can take time. It is unreasonable to expect a plan in just a few hours.
* Let the colorist be creative to provide interesting and practical options.

The color specialist often begins the working relationship by having the client complete a detailed color profile that pinpoints color preferences in an analytical way with evaluations on lifestyle, personality and more. Once hired, the specialist will advise not only about color choice but also about paint finishes, for example, satin vs. semi-gloss paint on the trim.

Why use a specialist? Jacobs cites an example of a historic home from the late 1800s in Cambridge, Massachusetts. After an expensive restoration, the owners chose a yellow body color with a 1950s feel. The job had to be redone. Attaining the right shade can be difficult. Hiring an expert might have saved a costly mistake.

House colors can be tricky to select. Work with a color specialist to choose a color scheme you'll be satisfied with for years to come.

The Big Decision

"Color – exterior color in particular – is often an afterthought in the design process. But it should not be so," according to Barbara Jacobs. "Exterior colors can be combined in subtle or bold combinations to communicate visual messages such as exuberance or elegance. Regardless of the type of building, exterior color creates a first – and lasting – impression."

Before a paintbrush is lifted, you'll need to know your neighborhood restrictions. Many of us live within the jurisdiction of homeowners' associations (HOA) and Historic Preservation Overlay Zones (HPOZ) that can be – to use a common expression -- both a blessing and a curse. While these groups prevent mayhem, they can also inhibit expressionism. When working with an HOA or HPOZ, be sure you understand and follow their process and regulations on color palettes to avoid fines, wasted money and effort, and the ire of your neighbors.

To help get you started, break color selection down into a step-by-step process:

Deep red on both the exterior and interior doors punches up the color of this home's front space. Even city homes and brownstones, which are often characterized by non-changeable brick facades, offer opportunities for personal touches through creative door and window trim colors. *Photo by Nancy Fay*

The intensity of this chartreuse door makes this historic town-house a stand-out on the block. *Photo by Nancy Fay*

* Identify the color elements of your landscape that won't change, such as the roof, stonework or driveway. These pre-existing materials will be the impetus from which your color scheme will emerge.
* Define your need for accent colors. Will you draw attention to specific architectural details or down-play others (like gutters)? Dark colors will make elements recede and appear smaller; their lighter counterparts will make them come forward and appear larger. An intense, vibrant, or rich hue, such as terracotta or eggplant, will imbue a detail with instant notability.
* Take a digital photograph of your home. If you are computer savvy, use photo editing software to experiment manipulate and change the exterior color electronically until you achieve a look you like.
* Or, take a regular photograph of your home. Enlarge it on a color copier and make several copies. Use tracing paper, watercolors, colored pencils or markers to try different themes.

This traditional Craftsman goes modern with chocolate brown and crisp white.

Subtle shades of blue, taupe and cream in the stonework are balanced by the muted tones of the fencing and trim work.

An expanse of coral brightens the appearance of a humble garage.

* Take into consideration the homes on either side of yours, as well as the general vibe of the neighborhood. An eclectic street of artsy bungalows can withstand bolder color schemes than a stately upscale traditional enclave.
* To simplify the process, refer to manufacturer-offered booklets that suggest palettes in various themes: historical, retro, traditional, Victorian, Craftsman.
* Or, to create your own combinations, purchase fans of color strips (costing between $10 and $20) that represent all colors within a paint line.
* Take an opinion poll from family and friends; though don't get overwhelmed by the diversity of response you're sure to receive.

The Palette

Once you've narrowed in on palette options for the exterior finish, trim and windows, buy sample sizes of the colors to test directly on the house. Study the combinations over the course of a week, and at varying times of day, to observe how light conditions will affect them. Paint will fade over time (particularly the darker shades) so you might want to choose the next shade deeper than your intended choice.

Choosing the palette can be an exciting adventure. Experiment with various color combinations on a practice board before making your final decision, and view colors in varying light throughout the day.

Stone's natural variations can stimulate your selection of trim colors. This façade inspired the blue-on-blue color combination.

For direction on where to place your house colors, look to the architecture for clues. Historically, a change in material usually indicates a change in color. A basic rule of thumb is to create a three-color scheme: one for the body of the house and two or more accents for doors, windows and trim. Jolino Beserra, an L.A. based designer and mosaic artist, recalls a sophisticated color combination he created for a client's 1930s Spanish bungalow. "The house had been plain beige with no accent for years. My clients wanted an artistic yet elegant color scheme to add personality and play up architectural details. I chose a warm, crisp green for the base that played off the terra cotta roof tiles, and a cool turquoise accent around the natural-stained wood windows. Since the majority of the house was warm-toned, the juxtaposition of the cool accent made the color combination come alive."

The three-color palette will give your home dimension and nuance, especially when you consider that visible building materials (roof shingles, brick, stone, etc.) add even more variety to the mix. Looking for a more understated effect? Experiment with quiet mossy greens, taupe and a splash of eggplant for drama. A skilled eye is needed for a more complicated color scheme, like that of an ornamented Victorian. In that case, your best option may be to hire a color specialist to design a standout combination.

Beserra encourages taking chances with color. "People are so afraid of it, but it's all about creating balance. One of my clients clung to white, but their artwork spoke of a different story. I wrapped them in soft lavenders and greens. They were shocked to discover how much they loved it. It didn't overwhelm them." Many striking color combinations can be conceived without white. Why not try a dark neutral such as chocolate, deep taupe or slate? *Experiment.*

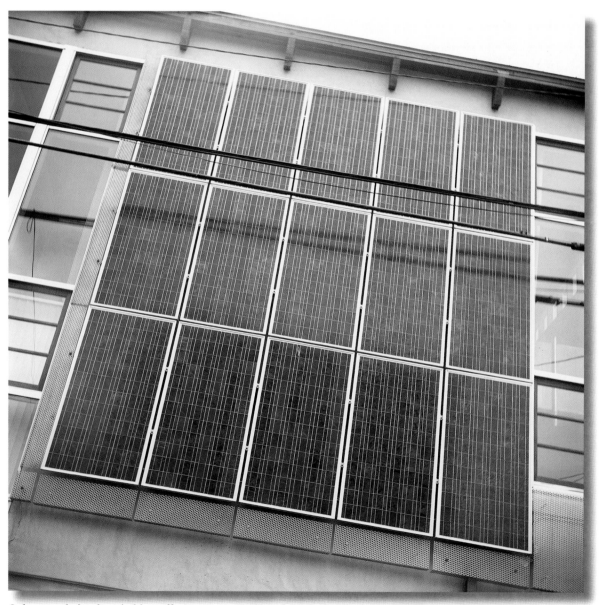

Solar panels in electric blue offer energy-conscious function and a bold design statement.

Past Meets Present

Older homes become quickly refreshed when colors are updated. In this renovation of a stately Craftsman, a washed-out palette of dull grey and white was replaced with this sage green and cream combination, inspired by the owner's childhood home.

Historical paints were founded on natural tints – the white of chalk dust, the red of cranberry dye, the green of leaves. In fact, research reveals that thousands of years ago semi-precious stones were used to create bright blue, red, yellow and green paints. Vitruvius described production of white lead and verdigris as early as the 2nd century AD. Now computer technology can recreate history through paint.

If you're working with a period home and want to recreate its original hue, a pro can color-match using an original paint sample hidden beneath more recent paint jobs. Unless undertaking strict restoration, most homeowners are satisfied with historically appropriate color palettes, derived from resource books and heritage paint lines. Historians have done a superb job researching and archiving past color trends.

Do you have to stay true to history or can you inject your own modern sense of color style? Color Specialist Barbara Jacobs points to the homeowners of San Francisco's painted ladies as an example of historic interpretation with a contemporary vernacular. "Lots of architectural detail, highlighted by bright or high contrast colors, is a modern concept of what a Victorian should look like. The original paint was not so bright for exterior colors. Style was in part a product of current trends and the materials available at the time."

Author Michelle Valigursky creates a visual design board before every major renovation project. "Use an 11x14" or larger piece of foam core, and mount on it a sketch of your home and yard. Build your landscaping and curb appeal plan from there, using representative paint chips, material samples, flower petals, fabric swatches, and more. When it's time to meet with contractors, this visual reference guide will eliminate confusion."

Landscaping Color

You've put thought into your curb appeal decisions. You'll still need to address color in your home's landscaping so the front exterior, as a whole, is unified. Landscape Designer Judy Kameon uses her insights into her client's preferences and personality when introducing color into her landscapes. "It's important for me to respond to the palette people have inside their homes. If someone loves earth tones, I won't give them a hot pink and orange garden. I'll give them a neutral garden with a bit of an accent."

For a Pasadena bungalow, the accent color she chose was gold. "We brought in gold alstramarias, which are like a lily, and some gold kangaroo paw, a grasslike plant. We did several shades of yellows and gold and cranked up the palette. We added white roses and these beautiful, mustard glazed pots as accents. The client loved it."

Jolino Beserra often looks to the vibrant colors of his Indian-Mexican heritage for inspiration. "A friend's Mexican folk art collection initially inspired me to connect with my roots. I loved the vibrant colors in the folk art tradition and realized that they were present and in harmony with nature." Soon, they started to make their way into his garden designs -- the daring yet harmonious combinations of vivid greens, blues, pinks, purples, and oranges have come to be emblematic of Beserra's design signature.

Landscape Designer Randy Anderson makes an important point to consider. While house colors are constant, landscape color is in a state of continual change. "I design my landscapes so that color is always present. I incorporate flowering shrubs with varying bloom times, particularly those that flower more than once like the Encore Azalea, and deciduous plants and trees that display striking color even after the leaves have fallen, such as the deep purple stems of Virginia Sweetspire. Add in early-spring bulbs and trees that give a gorgeous fall display and you'll always have great color to anticipate year round."

The hardscape elements of a home's exteriors can also be influenced by color. In addition to the natural soft grey and brown of stone and slate, concrete and other aggregates can also add a punch of color to a setting through addition of powder or liquid pigment. This material is also a good choice when the climate is prone to repeated freezing and thawing. Color Specialist Barbara Jacobs collaborated with Massachusetts Architect David Sharff on an exterior home renovation of a traditional shingle style Cape Cod in which the stained concrete driveway became one of its most striking features. Individual concrete pavers resembling cobblestones were tinted nuanced shades of eggplant, echoing the color scheme Jacobs created for the house.

Against a clean white façade, multi-colored florals and greenery add drama.

Landscape designer Judy Kameon uses a monochromatic approach that relies on gold-hued plantings and mustard glazed pots to create a soothing front garden for her client. *Photo by Eric Otsea*

Plantings like the red banana tree were chosen to accent the eggplant trim and wall color on author Lisa Vail's cottage renovation. *Photo by Costa Singer*

Hot pink florals pop when set against the deep blue background of the home's exterior.

Accessories offer unique opportunities to add jolts of color as seen here in mosaic artist Jo Beserra's sleeping figure. *Photo by Jo Beserra*

The rectilinear lines of city homes can be softened with a resplendent sidewalk cutting garden in soft, complementary hues.

Window boxes offer a perfect opportunity to create a mini-garden of color against the solid surface of your home.

Hydrangeas come in a variety of shades ranging from white to pale green to vibrant pink and electric blue.

Gardeners can manipulate the shades of hydrangeas by experimenting with nutrients. The addition of dolomitic lime will result in a pink bloom, while aluminum sulfate will force the blooms to deeper shades of blue. White hydrangeas, however, will only show a blush of natural pink, no matter how the soil is altered. *Photo by Michelle Valigursky*

Hot red clematis cascades over a white fence for contrast.

This home's neutral palette gets jolts of vivid color through blue glazed ceramic pots and red geraniums.

The Curb Appeal Perspective: A World of Color

Find colorful inspiration in public like this field of fountain grass at St. James Bay, Florida. Planting large expanses of a single color can make a powerful statement. *Photo by Michelle Valigursky*

Driveways offer an opportunity for colorful expression with tinted concrete, brick and stone that reinforce the palette.

Historically, a change in exterior material dictated a color change.

We've all seen the occasional turquoise house, or the Colonial with the bright door that isn't exactly a pleasing shade of red, or the yellow Cape Cod more neon than sunshine. Somewhere between the paint chip and the house, the color envisioned gets lost in translation.

Choosing colors can be difficult, especially when it comes to showcasing architecture. In his book *Your House: The Outside View,* author John Prizeman notes, "Painting a house is like taking a huge communal picture in which the rest of the painting is either done by nature or by other people. It is not static; it changes with the time of day, the seasons, and the plantings. It has the power to enhance or mar the overall scene."

So, should you play it safe? Or take a chance to let your inner artist shine?

When it comes to resale, California Real Estate Agent Katherine Davis acknowledges "most people don't have the imagination for change. Buyers have said, 'I love this house but I just couldn't live with the color!' It never occurs to them they can change it. This is all the more reason to have a professional designer choose your color scheme."

But she delivers a word of caution. With bolder color choices, "you take a risk of turning off buyers, no matter how well it's done. It will take a special buyer to love it and feel the color scheme fits their personality. If the paint needs to be changed, buyers will deduct the expense by offering less money for the house."

Atlanta Real Estate Agent Sharon Cunningham concurs. "When I list a house with an outdated or inappropriate color scheme, I strongly encourage the sellers to have it painted before it goes on the market. Yes, it is a big upfront investment but I assure them it will pay off on the backend." Cunningham debunks the myth that buyers would rather make color decisions themselves. "On the contrary, the homes that sell the fastest and for the most money are those that have had all the right design choices implemented already."

"To this I can attest: one of the best deals I ever got was on a 1930s Spanish home painted an unfortunate aqua blue," Author Lisa Vail recalls. "No one wanted to buy 'The Toothpaste House' and it lingered on the market for months. Since I can see beyond such easily fixable problems, I bought the house considerably below market value."

Prizeman takes this point a step further by evaluating climate. He says, "What colors can you use? Does your area have bright sunny skies? If so, you can paint the house in brighter hues, like the Mediterranean. If your area has mainly cool, grey skies, your color choices will be affected."

Real Estate Agent's Rule: Match color choices to building material and geography. Icing colors for gingerbread trim may work fine on San Francisco Victorians, but typical suburban buyers expect subtlety. Be inspired, but balance the colors against the unchangeable and natural elements of your home's surround.

Architect Michael Hricak's former cottage in Venice, California was reconfigured with steel, Texas limestone and a mix of inexpensive off-the-shelf vinyl and commercial-grade windows.

Chapter Five
Doors and Windows

Legendary Modern Architect Louis Sullivan once talked about how "form follows function." His work influenced protégée Frank Lloyd Wright, who clarified his mentor's concept: "Form and function should be one, joined in a spiritual union." This Wrightian philosophy encapsulates how we think of an exceptional home's doors and windows--as a perfect marriage between form and function. At their best, windows frame pleasant views, provide light and ventilation while protecting us from the elements. They define architectural style. At their worst, they are poorly sited, inefficient and detract from a home's overall aesthetic.

The front door is the most prominent entrance to a house, and should provide a convenient entry for family and an appealing destination point for visitors. All too often, however, doors appear out of character with the rest of the home, are in disrepair, or are so nondescript that newcomers have trouble finding them at all.

The right doors and windows are critical components for achieving curb appeal; without their finishing touch, a truly attractive home front remains elusive. Now more than ever, a plethora of styles, materials and price points is available to radically rejuvenate your home's façade. So which are best for your home? While no hard and fast rules dictate style, understanding the home's architecture and site will ensure doors and windows successfully enhance the front façade, rather than clash with it.

Contemporary homes tend to look best with large, metal or wood-framed casement and awning windows with single panes that blur the division of inside and out. Unadorned steel doors allowed to oxidize over time and the painted wood slab style made popular by architect Joseph Eichler are perfectly at home on the Mid-Century Modern.

New home construction blends the best of technology and design in doors and windows. *Photo by Lisa Vail*

Traditional homes and colonial architecture look in sync with divided light windows in six-over-six or eight-over-eight panes and a variety of door designs that reflect the old-world charm of your home's particular era. High-end door manufacturers offer fiberglass options with convincing wood grains and detailed architectural panels that easily pass for old-world craftsmanship while adding safety, energy efficiency, and weather resistance.

The muted palette of the roof is balanced by the washed wood door and window of this California cottage. *Photo by Michelle Valigursky*

All points lead to this lovely entry, with a covered portico and iron light fixtures that complement the railings. Architectural history is reflected in both doors and windows. *Photo by Michelle Valigursky*

The sleek simplicity of this slab-front door with sidelite supports the rectilinear presentation of the breezeway.

Making a Grand Entrance

Doors can be as distinctive as their owners, especially when leaded glass, antique hardware, or decorative metalwork are incorporated. Atlanta Street of Dreams Designer Euna Williams believes the front door affords homeowners a perfect opportunity for artistic expression. "When building or renovating a home, the door should be a focal point," she explains. "It's important that the door, transom windows and side lites complement the home's architecture. But complementary doesn't have to mean predictable."

While customizing a front door to your own specifications tends to be expensive, this just might be the place to spend extra renovation dollars if a truly distinctive entry is your fantasy. "Using forged iron and leaded glass, artisans translate my designs into unique works of art," says Williams. "My clients have made contemporary expressions and reflections of Art Deco. Whatever their taste, we create one-of-a-kind doors that are both eye-catching and functional."

Even traditionalists enjoy differentiating their home from those of their neighbors. This can be accomplished through the use of salvage pieces. Sometimes a well-chosen architectural feature added to your home's entryway can make all the difference. Tapered columns, an umbrella awning, a pergola roof, an ironwork canopy or a stone archway take an ordinary front façade from ordinary to extraordinary.

The rustic wood of this decorative door is enhanced by a simple scroll of ironwork.

A renovated traditional home gets a polished look with textured glass and wood doors. *Photo by Michelle Valigursky*

Brilliant colors shine in the leaded glass of the front door.

This artistic English antique door sets an inviting tone for this eclectic historic cottage.

A whimsical doorbell gives visitors a reason to smile.

Broad steps invite visitors up to the double doors in a welcoming approach to this home.

The classic red door beckons entrance to the arbor.

A boldly painted door will add drama to your home's front space.

Contrasting paint colors highlight the architectural design of this historic door. *Photo by Nancy Fay*

To Replace or Not to Replace

In older city homes, form and function go hand in hand with decorative iron panels that also serve as security bars.

In a historic or city home, windows serve double duty as garden spaces.

In neighborhoods with historic homes, potential buyers usually prize original wood windows. "Too often, I've seen uninformed homeowners rip out the old windows and replace them with inexpensive vinyl ones," laments Jesus Sanchez of the Los Angeles Echo Park Historical Society, one of many organizations dedicated to the preservation of our country's oldest neighborhoods. "They soon realize their mistake when they put the house back on the market. Buyers looking for architectural authenticity are turned off. They either don't bid, or will offer a much lower price."

In the 1960s and 1970s, homeowners often replaced original windows with louvered ones known as jalousies. These were supposed to be breezy in the summer, but inadvertently let in cool air during the winter months, as well. Besides being extremely inefficient, they are unattractive and impossible to keep clean. Author Lisa Vail points out, "During the renovation of a 1930s Spanish bungalow, we replaced jalousies with double-hung, single-paned wood windows from Marvin. It cost approximately $7,000, but the difference in the home's curb appeal, sound reduction and energy efficiency was worth the expense. When we sold, we easily earned back our investment."

Architect David Sharff deals with window replacement often in his renovation projects, especially when additions are involved. "For a high-end window, which I would use on both new and period houses, Pella or Marvin offer detail options which come close to historical wood windows. Small window manufacturers also specialize in matching historic structures." For maintenance purposes, many of Sharff's clients request a clad window, available in vinyl, aluminum or warranted factory paint finishes in custom colors. He adds, "Window technology has perfected the simulated divided light product which gives an insulated window and permanently applied detailed muntins on both the interior and exterior. However, nothing comes close to an original single glazed true divided light window. I specify those for homeowners interested in historical accuracy."

Sanchez suggests another option besides manufacturer-bought windows. "If your older home has already lost its original windows to a past renovation, hire a local craftsman to reproduce the window style that suits the home's age and architecture. Oftentimes, other houses in your neighborhood will have been built during the same time period, even by the same builder, and can offer clues into what your windows originally looked like."

In this charming cottage, mini-pane windows offer an unexpected surprise in this home's front space. *Photo by Michelle Valigursky*

The arched garage door is topped by a peaked roof and petite shuttered window.

These custom-made wood shutters were an integral part of this mid-century ranch's Old World-style transformation.

The addition of a Juliet balcony can add drama to the planes of your home. *Photo by Michelle Valigursky*

Advances in Window Technology

When glass windows first hit the American residential scene in the early 1700s, glass had to be imported from England, making them an unaffordable luxury to all but the wealthiest colonists. The rudimentary single-hung windows were comprised of small individual panes of glass held in place by wood framing known as muntins.

By the end of the 19th century, American glassworks made glass windows accessible to the average homeowner, and continual technological advances allowed for larger expanses of glass and fewer windowpanes. Twelve-over-twelve lite configurations evolved to 9-over-9, then to the 6-over-6 that is still popular today. Eventually, glass became so strong that

While they may look the part of yesteryear's windows, these boast the latest in technology such as low-e and argon-filled glass.

leads to a lower U-Value, which measures energy loss through conduction and infiltration (the lower the number, the better). The opposite is R-Value, which measures how resistant a material is to heat flow (the higher the number, the better). Manufacturers add argon gas to fill the space between panes to insulate, and others apply a pyrolytic coating to second or third surfaces to increase solar heat gain.

But don't assume that full-fledged window replacement is the only solution for energy conservation. Well-crafted and well-cared-for original wood windows on an older home should be treasured. A number of products in the marketplace can improve their effectiveness while maintaining high aesthetic standards, such as:

* *"Invisible" aluminum storm windows*—Mounted inside or out, these barely-noticeable storm windows achieve energy savings, noise reduction and UV reduction without masking the appearance of historic windows.

Windows on this modern home are thoughtfully placed to maximize light.

large, uninterrupted panes could be sustained within a frame without internal support.

Our early window-makers would be amazed by how far their industry has come. Today, manufacturers offer insulated and low-e coated products for noise reduction, energy efficiency and ultraviolet reduction. Frames come in an array of materials besides wood, including vinyl, fiberglass, aluminum and combination frames. Window types for every architectural style and personal preference are readily available, from the virtual glass "walls" of the ultra-modern to reproductions of Victorian, Prairie and Craftsman-era stained glass.

Suffice it to say that a major benefit to window replacement is the improved energy conservation new technology provides. The government has created the ENERGY-STAR® program to identify windows and doors that qualify as high-efficiency. Simply put, low-e means low emissivity. The glass is coated with a thin metallic oxide layer that reflects interior heat back into a building in cooler months, and prevents heat from entering the building during hotter seasons. This

This sleek garage door echoes the streamlined design of the house.

Angled shutters allow breezes to ventilate this home's screened porch.

* *Disappearing screens*—Made for windows and doors, these screens pull out when needed and remain out of sight when not. Keeps bugs out so you can enjoy fresh air, *sans* air conditioning.
* *Window tinting*—Avoid sun-faded upholstery, lightened wood floors and overheated rooms by having professionals apply this thin film to window glass.
* *Retractable awnings*—Stock styles are available in weather-resistant fabrics, though they can also be custom-made. Allows the sun to warm the interior spaces in the winter months and provides shade in the summer.

If you are concerned about energy loss from your original single-paned windows, or if seal failure has occurred on your older double panes, consider having the glass replaced by a reputable window glass company. The cost difference is significantly lower than installing a new window and it is a great option if the window frame itself is in good repair. It is also a good idea to replace old glass if you have children in your home, since the tempered glass used today is far safer should it break.

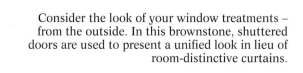

Consider the look of your window treatments – from the outside. In this brownstone, shuttered doors are used to present a unified look in lieu of room-distinctive curtains.

The Curb Appeal Perspective: Keep Them Clean!

Symmetry in window placement achieves balance on the home front.

When a house is on the market, people usually remember to mow the lawn and pick up trash. But they often overlook sprucing up windows and doors. Pat Dumon, a real estate agent from New Bern, North Carolina, suggests the following:

* Remove and store out of sight all window screens from the home's front space.
* Thoroughly wash windows until they sparkle. Hire a professional service for the best results.
* Inspect the front door for peeling paint, dulled varnish, scuff marks and chips. Touch up as necessary. When in doubt, hire a professional to ensure the correct products are used to do the job.
* Replace the doorbell fixture with something fresh, up to date, interesting and tasteful. It's a quick fix that may be the first item a buyer touches in your home.
* Polish all fixtures and kick plates until they gleam.
* By all means, replace broken windowpanes and glass.
* Remove security doors and bars from windows. They give the impression that your neighborhood is unsafe.
* Replace handle and lock hardware if no longer in good repair. Nothing is more frustrating for a real estate agent than struggling to open the front door for their clients.

Real Estate Agent's Rule: Sparkling windows and polished doors translate into a better first impression: a seller's attention to cleanliness and repair details speak well of the state of the home. The small investment you make in window cleaning and door polishing may come back to you in the form of a lucrative sales contract.

This wood door adds natural beauty and also acts as an effective insulator.

Attention to detail and cleanliness will be appreciated by even the most finicky homebuyer.

Planting en masse defines a landscape through areas of repetition and volume.

Chapter Six
Lush Landscapes

The backyard has long been the bastion of great landscape design, with terraces, gazebos, waterfalls and natural rock formations nestled amongst woodland gardens and beds of sun-loving flora. But we believe the same finesse should be applied to the home's front landscape with gardens that could inspire a Monet masterpiece.

Landscape designer Randy Anderson takes an inside-out approach and thinks outside the traditional front yard box. As Anderson says, "I create multi-dimensional gardens just as pleasurable to view from inside the house as from the street." He adds, "While a specific view may need to be blocked, why cut off attractive 'borrowed' views in the process? Break up the design so you screen only where needed."

The trend toward a straight row of foundation plantings flanking a straight path seems to be fading away. This dull trend initiated as a camouflage for unattractive concrete block foundations. When done right, however, foundation plants can draw your eye to the door, play up attractive architectural features, downplay flaws and unite the home with the surrounding landscape.

Whether you're taking cues from the English Arts and Crafts gardens of Gertrude Jekyll and Edwin Lutyens, or giving life to one of your own design, landscape should evolve with the seasons in an ever-changing display of color, texture, line and dimension.

Sustainable landscaping utilizes indigenous and imported plants that easily acclimate to a region. These water-friendly grasses of varying heights and textures replace the typical front lawn.

Lush variations in foliage create a dazzling display in all types of gardens. *Photo by Michelle Valigursky*

Foundation plantings create a focal point in the architecture where none existed previously. *Photo by Nancy Fay*

Begin with Design – and Budget

When setting a remodel or new construction budget, set aside funds for landscaping to complete your home's presentation. Architect Scott West and Atlanta landscape design firm Tokikata Modern Gardens collaborated on this modern home's front spaces to create a Zen-Modern aesthetic.

Nearly all professionals we talked with agree that the first step in creating a memorable landscape is to identify the type of design that will serve as the basis for the project. It's important to point out that even the pros work with pros to maximize ideas and choose the best.

Architect Miri Lerner almost always uses a landscape architect when she designs a home. "I'm taking into account the entire property. After all, the landscaping will be viewed from inside the house." Landscape Designer Judy Kameon says, "It's really important when we're first meeting prospective clients to find out their tastes. I like to see people's houses – inside. I want to know what kind of colors they like. I like to know plants they love, plants they hate. How much do they entertain? Do they want a living room environment? We ask starter questions then follow up with specifics to create the overall design concept."

Budgeting up front is critical. People often undertake a renovation project in stages. Even so, Architect David Sharff finds that landscaping expenditure tends to find its way to the bottom line of the budget. He gets discouraged when clients consider landscaping as a "down the line" project.

The homeowner has several options. Design and implement every phase of the plan himself, hire professionals to complete essential tasks and supervise plan implementation, or offer personal suggestions then step back to leave the entire job to the pros. Even if you don't finish the on-paper planning, sketching out a few quick ideas will be a beneficial point of reference for the landscape designer you may hire.

River rock and smaller stones are the perfect ground cover for this walled succulent garden.

Cast concrete stepping stones will have you visually skipping across a Japanese-inspired pond in this botanical garden. *Photo by Michelle Valigursky*

Shared yard space can benefit the community with a garden planted and tended to by all residents. *Photo by Michelle Valigursky*

A refined garden was created around a water feature that is enjoyed both indoors and out. *Photo by Michelle Valigursky*

Flowing or Formal – What's Your Style?

Whether your home is an ultra-hip Seattle modern or a Michigan lakeside cabin, maintain landscape continuity with the details of the house and neighborhood. An asymmetrical house offers more freedom in plant selection and placement, with specific natural elements balancing the architectural features. For example, espaliered camellias may engage a blank wall to complement an important window or striations of Mexican heather could break up an expanse of lawn.

"We work on architecturally significant houses. Some of those clients want a graphic, architectural aesthetic to reflect the house," says Landscape Designer Judy Kameon. "Then again, others want to go against type. With an austere, minimal house they might want a wild, lush garden counterpart to that."

So how does Kameon decide what type of garden to implement? It's a give-and-take process with the client that often involves re-education. If a client has a Spanish house but wants a Japanese garden, she might suggest, "a look that works with the home yet also has the essence that attracts the homeowner to the Japanese gardens. In one case, to marry the two styles, I gave them a modern cottage-style garden. Moments were quiet and simple, where everything was green on green. With such an unfussy design, we satisfied that desire for tranquility."

"If a client loves a certain plant that doesn't fit the site requirements, we substitute one that evokes a similar feel through texture, color and shape," says Randy Anderson. Sun-loving creeping juniper might be swapped for pachysandra in a shady yard.

Thanks to former First Lady Ladybird Johnson, wildflower gardens are an American trend on highways and hillsides. While naturalized flowers may be a tempting solution for a hilly front yard, Landscape Designer Jenn Carr points out, "Wildflowers are too much upkeep for the average person. Perhaps the bigger downside is that they don't look great for a large part of the year."

Garden design should not intimidate. While being a purist has its benefits, perhaps the most successful landscape plans do not stick to the "rules" of any one design type. Instead they mix and match complementary elements of each until personal style is defined in an aesthetically expressive way.

Every landscape design needs a focal point. Position a stone bench or an iron sculpture in a key location to draw the eye. From that critical point, the visitor's gaze will travel to other elements in the immediate surrounds. But manipulate space to maximize impact. Add mystery to a narrow garden with a curving path to divide space. Plant perennials or compact shrubs at one curve to shield what lays beyond.

And here's a tip if your garden is particularly shallow. Elongate the space by incorporating design lines that run from house to street: a colonnade of small trees, a low hedge or a path that narrows slightly toward the house.

Cutting gardens of blooms are possible in even the smallest of garden spaces such as out front of this in-town home.

In this front landscape by Landscape Designer Judy Kameon, plants with height were chosen near the front patio to create privacy while slow growing lavender softens the path's hard angles. *Photo by Eric Otsea*

This stylish city space smartly incorporates a combination of landscaping techniques, including container gardening, window boxes and conventional planting beds.

Grasses and clusters of wildflowers work companionably in an approach garden near a home's entrance.

Architectural design features can be greatly enhanced by placement of a brilliant-hued hanging or container garden.

Plant flowers for their color and bloom time as well as their ability to attract the wildlife you admire.

Do your homework on varieties of bamboo, as some may run rampant in your garden space. Bamboo is well-suited to container gardening. *Photo by Michelle Valigursky*

Resist the Invaders

Though it might be intriguing to plant fast-growing ground cover, think twice. Many communities have banned the planting of invasive vines that rapidly destroy woodlands and are injurious to gardens. Carefully monitor or avoid the following: English ivy, kudzu, morning glory, Chinese wisteria, euonymus, Japanese honeysuckle, porcelain berry, mile-a-minute and creeping fig.

Consider instead the ecologically-friendly myrtle, pachysandra, mahonia, liriope and ajuga. For the health of your garden, keep the invaders at bay. That also means running bamboo, which can quickly spread out of control.

Streetscapes, Parkways and Neutral Grounds

Some call it the parkway. Others call it a streetscape. Down South it's no-man's land or the neutral ground. No matter what it's called in your neck of the woods, city homes often feature space between sidewalk and street that lends homeowners a fine opportunity for showcasing garden design. Before a visitor to your home even enters your yard, he'll already taste your style by viewing the design concept you've put in place on this borrowed land.

In some municipalities, keeping up these areas is required. In others, it's forbidden. Know which rules you are bound to obey. In addition, call the city before you dig to review setback and sightline requirements and to mark cable, phone, water, and gas lines. For precautionary reasons, plants must not uproot sidewalks or overflow onto the sidewalk or street.

Randy Anderson offers advice on planting trees near the street and neighboring properties. "Keep the ultimate spread in mind when planting trees. I've heard fussing between neighbors when one's tree encroaches on another's property, especially if the tree is messy." Many a lawyer has handled disputes over damages that occur in exactly these instances.

To prevent foundation, pathway, driveway and hardscape damage by infiltrating roots, plant trees in appropriate locations. Anderson points out, "It would be sad to think a future owner will have your beloved tree removed because it wasn't given enough room to grow."

Clean, simple and elegant, this stucco wall becomes the perfect backdrop to a sidewalk garden of succulents and annuals.

Take care when selecting plants for a planting bed bordered by a sidewalk as many can quickly become high maintenance.

The fescue grass and boulder design makes the jump from private to public property to create a seamless presentation from curb to home.

Xeriscaping and Conservation

This dry riverbed not only offers a lovely aesthetic but also provides a functional solution to runoff.

A stone and moss path makes ambling through a mature Southwestern garden enticing.

Water is a finite resource, and landscape designers are acutely aware of the need to create designs that conserve natural resources. The term "Xeriscaping" is recent, but the practice of planting the topography to maximize the use of water is centuries old.

"You don't have to use yuccas and cacti everywhere to practice environmentally-friendly gardening," says Randy Anderson. "Common sense dictates plant choice. Azaleas in full sun require excessive water to keep them alive. Grass on steep slopes encourages water runoff. Choose plant life to complement conditions."

Understand that automatic sprinklers are not always the most efficient way to water. "This encourages perennial weeds to grow around plants," Anderson says. "Grass doesn't need to be watered every day. It's essential for the landscaper to properly prepare the soil so grass can develop deep roots. The homeowner must water only when necessary to develop drought tolerancy."

A modern townhome's tiny plot of plantable space has plenty of drama thanks to stone orbs dotted among the drought-tolerant plantings.

Xeriscaping minimizes maintenance and conserves resources. This Virginia garden also uses it to create a place for contemplation when boulder seats are added to water-friendly border plants and chipped stone. *Photo by Michelle Valigursky*

This street-side garden belongs to an avid gardener who doesn't mind the deadheading, pruning and weeding that's required to keep perennials looking tidy.

Made in the Shade

Each woodland garden has subtle layers: a canopy of tall trees that shade a lower story of shrubs, which in turn protect low plantings like ferns and hostas, which hover over a final layer of groundcover. "In a woodland setting, the emphasis is on tranquility," Anderson says. "It's not about being showy."

For the best effect, Anderson recommends visiting woods and observing how nature lays out its plants. "Take plenty of pictures and notice the dappled or filtered light cast by lacy trees. These trees shield plants from direct sun while still admitting the light needed by most plants." And he notes, "A grove of canopy trees under-planted with azaleas and other shade-tolerant plants makes a natural, low-maintenance setting that attracts birds and other wildlife."

If evergreens dominate your property, remember that "ferns, violets and other woodland varieties can handle full shade," Anderson explains. Half shade requires forethought in planning. "For instance, if you get shade in the afternoon, blooming plants such as begonias or impatiens will welcome the soft early sun but won't wither as the day's heat strengthens." Aesthetes can prompt the impression of sunlight even in a shady glen by selecting plants with variegated leaves.

On porches and patios where sun exposure is limited, container gardening is key because of flexibility in locating pots according to the sun cycles. However, Anderson reminds, "Avoid using too many small pots, which can clutter and confuse the picture."

Include seating in your landscape to enjoy your gardening efforts year-round.

A shady hillside is perfect for planting ferns, variegated hostas, coleus and ground cover.

The Curb Appeal Perspective:
First Impressions Mean Everything

To attract buyers to your home for sale, pay careful attention to the visual impact of your front space landscaping – it sets the first impression of your property and may influence buying decisions. The formal, English garden out front of this Colonial-style home alludes to what a homeowner can expect once inside.

For a do-it-yourself landscape renovation, ask plenty of questions at your local nursery or garden center. Experienced staff members can offer valuable advice and steer you toward greenery that works best in your area.

Perhaps the largest contributing factor to a buyer's first impression is the landscape. But the ability to recoup landscaping dollar investment is so subjective it has not been measured by the annual *Remodeling Magazine Cost vs. Value Report*. Real Estate Agent Laura Law points out, "It's hard to put a dollar amount on front yard landscaping. If you spend $50,000, you probably won't get an additional $50,000 in resale. It's not dollar for dollar, like a kitchen or bathroom would be," she says. "Of course, you do have to make your home appealing. It won't matter how nice your kitchen is if no one comes in and sees it."

She goes on to say, "If you already know your house will be back on the market in a few years, emulate the landscaping of the most sought-after properties in your neighborhood. You won't be landscaping for yourself, but for popular taste. But if this home will be yours indefinitely, do what makes you happy. You will recoup your investment in personal enjoyment."

California Investor and Real Estate Agent Michael Caldwell offers an opinion on floral installation. "If a property needs work on the inside, it's not going to help to put in $200 worth of plants at the last second," he says. "But if you hover in that gray area with a really nice house, plantings can move you up market."

Do blooms add to the value of a home? Real Estate Appraiser Sheridan Shaffer notes, "There is nothing like flowers. Even if you are broke, you can afford a flat or two from your local home improvement center." Shaffer knows that "buyers will be swayed by them, therefore making your house more marketable."

Landscape Designer Randy Anderson suggests sprucing up front yards for resale — lay new pine straw, plant annuals for highlight and color, cut edges, remove unhealthy plants and replace them. Occasionally, they are asked to replace foundation plants. "We don't usually recommend sellers put $20,000 worth of plants in at this point. People don't buy landscapes, they buy houses."

Anderson adds a bonus point. "However, if buyers pass a garden that's freshly done, they know the front landscaping is one less expense they'll have to deal with right away." When it comes to removing mature trees, he advises, "Don't be hasty. The right trees add value so don't take out a stately, well-placed tree just to grow grass."

Real Estate Agent's Rule: Make it beautiful. Make it green. Keep it well maintained. If you do, buyers will come inside.

Landscape designer Judy Kameon forces visitors to literally slow down and smell the roses by designing the front path of this cottage garden to circumvent a central axis point.

Chapter Seven
Access: Pathways and Driveways

When entering a Japanese tea garden, the guest leaves the everyday world to enter one of natural harmony and serenity. By passing over a series of steppingstones and meandering through artfully placed patches of moss to move deeper into the lush, green garden and toward a stone water feature, the metamorphic process of stress release is achieved.

Architect Miri Lerner names this phenomenon "The Celebration of Arrival." She explains "As you approach a home, a transition happens from public space, to semi-public space, to private space. It is very important to fully experience that transition, not to hurry it." Do you experience this gentle shifting of perspective upon wandering through the pathways of your home's front space?

A property may be fronted by a path that reflects the architectural style and lines of the home.

Left:
Sculptural New Zealand flax defines a perfectly aligned concrete paver path to create a very modern aesthetic.

In Lisa Vail's own home, "the path is comprised of stone slabs embedded in a "sea" of Mexican beach rock. The configuration sets the tone for the surrounding contemplative garden and encourages visitors to slow down and enjoy the plantings."

We've all heard the aphorism that the fastest way from point A to point B is as the crow flies, yet design principles teach us the fastest way may also be the least attractive or inviting. We prefer instead angles and curves and stopping points -- elements of interest on a path or driveway that add spark and dimension to one of a home's essential front yard functions.

Problem Solving and Primary Paths

Before we can address aesthetics, we must first examine functional requirements such as drainage and grading. Landscape Designer Randy Anderson says, "No matter how great a landscaping concept looks, if it doesn't work functionally it will become a nightmare for homeowners. Water shouldn't flow toward a foundation or pool on walkways." He suggests the installation of French drains or gravel basins and hard liners beneath stone walkways to carry drainage water down and out of the area.

Once these issues are resolved, primary pathway design should enhance and complement the home's architecture. Primary paths should utilize solid materials like concrete, flagstone, brick or pavers, while secondary paths can be more *avant garde* and employ pea gravel, bark, mown grass or steppingstones edged by creeping thyme or Corsican mint. Scale should be in proportion to the home.

"Before finalizing a path, remember visitors to your home, and consider the safety of everyone from toddlers to grandparents. Is it an easy path to navigate in all weather and at different times of day?" asks Author Michelle Valigursky. "When choosing materials, consider how the path will be to maintain in all seasons."

Gullies on a property can transform from a detriment to key design choice when a custom-built bridge becomes a charming part of the arrival experience.

Stone steps flanked by boulders and potted annuals replace typical hillside landscaping.

Angles or Curves?

A path doesn't have to curve to be visually stimulating. Straight-edged paths balance homes with rectilinear lines. But instead of cutting straight up the yard, a walkway might zigzag to the front door, with landscaping or screens keeping what's around the corner a mystery waiting to be discovered.

Architect Miri Lerner designs her front walkways to include changes in direction. "You see the door, you want to approach it. You want to get closer, but as you do, you start finding yourself enjoying the process of getting there. You know where you're going, the direction is always clear, but little surprises and detours are along the way. A turn of the path, an interesting piece of artwork, beautiful landscaping. It's like a dance towards the front door."

Design Psychologist Susan Lee Painter describes the half-hidden path as a psychological image people find appealing. "It is not knowing where the path leads that we find so compelling on a basic level. We feel brave. It's an adventure to explore. It takes courage to go down the path and that is exciting on a primal level."

A flowering arbor at the entrance to a path is a welcome invitation. *Photo by Michelle Valigursky*

Architect Miri Lerner recommends, allow your visitors to enjoy the process of arriving at your home by providing turns in the path and points of interest along the way.

The Road Most Traveled

When homeowners consider renovations, altering the look of the driveway is a simple way to dramatically change a home's exterior. Texas Real Estate Agent Kelly Thate has spotted a trend of late. "Many homeowners and builders are using stained and scored concrete and exposed aggregate or bubble rock pavers so the driveway becomes more of a design feature, rather than a massive expanse of concrete."

Consider using a permeable paving surface, such as gravel and pervious concrete or asphalt to help mitigate the negative impact driveways and streets have on our environment. In urban and suburban areas, so much is paved that rainwater can no longer soak into the ground, as it should. Instead, it's forced into storm drains, picking up oil and chemicals before ending up in our rivers, lakes and coastal waters. Open-celled pavers and brick planted with hearty drought-tolerant grass make a soft presentation while allowing water to absorb into the soil underneath.

Entry markers, such as pillars, arches and gates can define a home's tone from first sight. In Seattle, "Upper end homes often have ornamental gates with lighted columns and security systems," says Real Estate Agent Pam Brossard. "These elements give visual interest to what might otherwise be an ordinary driveway." Besides being ornamental, entry markers let people know they've arrived, especially when house numbers are prominently displayed and the area is well lit. A beautiful specimen tree, planting beds or free-standing sections of fence can make your driveway entrance stand out to new visitors. Just be sure anything you place at the end of your drive doesn't obstruct your view of oncoming traffic.

So how do you determine driveway type and placement? Atlanta Architect Lorraine Enwright advises:

* *Understand local building codes.* Municipalities often regulate driveway angles with relation to the house.
* *Experiment with curved versus straight approaches.* Straight driveways can be steeper and more difficult to back out of, and may offer reduced visibility. Instead of straightaways, add flared and turnabout spaces.
* *Consider grade for sloped properties.* A gentle curve can make a driveway more manageable for both walking and driving.
* *Choose entry markers that complement your home's architecture.*
* *Limit plantings or opt for low-height specimens at critical visibility points.*
* *After a hard rain, check the water's path for runoff.* Does it collect in a corner or swell toward your garage door? Consider adding a drain to extend the life of your driveway.

Driveways can be as creative as any other element of your home. Here, the front lawn also becomes a "green" driveway when cement pavers are added to allow rain water to absorb into the ground.

Paving stones can be arranged in a variety of shapes to add visual interest to a driveway. Here, the drain becomes the center point of a circular pattern.

Driveways can reflect an era as in this brick-paved approach to a historic New York property.

Circular driveways eliminate the need for turnaround space while allowing for plenty or room for parking and play.

Marking the driveway with symmetrical, lighted pillars will define a home's entrance.

An allee of young trees will grow into a lush canopy over this driveway.

Steps

A required element in nearly every house, steps are considered functional necessities. However, many homeowners take pride in their aesthetic material interpretations and applications of materials such as custom-designed tile and forged iron accents.

Simple design rules apply to successful step construction. Repeating walkway materials will balance the front yard presentation, though introduction of new materials and railings can add color and dimension to the space.

* *Primary steps must be made of sturdy materials such as concrete, stone or brick.* Less-traveled secondary steps can be made of smooth boulders, railroad ties or gravel.
* *Steps should be at least four feet wide to allow two people to pass each other without bumping.*
* *Long flights of steps should be broken by landings, which can be terraces with garden seats and plantings.*
* *The tread to riser ratio must be safe.* Generally, four to seven inches high is satisfactory for the riser, with a 12-inch deep tread. Diverge from this and safety becomes an issue.

Ironwork railings can be as fanciful or artistic as the homeowner's taste.

Rustic steps are flanked by faux bois railings.

Hand-painted tile on the risers delights the eye when ascending the steps.

Pipe and wire edges these steps with industrial modernism.

Architect Lorraine Enwright used wide stone steps to create an inviting entrance to her home.

Bricks and Stones

Long gone are the days of dull concrete and tarry asphalt as our only choices for driveways and pathways. Now, more decorative choices abound.

* **Concrete:** Poured or pavers. All concrete can be tinted or stained to add a decorative element to your exterior color palette. Texture can be introduced. Concrete may also be mixed with aggregate for a multi-dimensional look.

* **Stone:** Traditional varieties include slate, bluestone and flagstone in all shapes and sizes. These can be found in irregular, natural shapes as well as more geometric pavers. A more exotic look is porphyry, cobblestone that throws off a bluish-purple or purple-red cast.

* **Rock:** Pebbles, decomposed granite, river rock, crushed gravel, pea gravel.

* **Brick:** Highly durable in a wide range of colors. These can be laid in a variety of patterns such as herringbone and basket weave.

Inventive homeowners find ways to combine materials to offer practicality and visual interest. One Atlanta homeowner conserved financial resources by using salvaged brick and concrete to shape her front courtyard and plant-edged path. The result was a striking blend of function and design.

Landscape Designer Jenn Carr lives in an enclave of historic homes where artists, designers and architects congregate. Recently, a new neighbor asked her advice about a broken brick path in a 1901 home. The homeowners wanted to preserve the path's character, but its deteriorated condition prevented complete salvage.

"For the do-it-yourselfer I'd recommend all materials be taken up and the surface leveled. Since this is an involved project, time must be invested on researching how to re-lay a brick path," she recommends. "I asked them to consider the option of re-digging the path trench and working around tree roots. In this case, the best solution would be to start from scratch and redesign the home's complete approach."

Carr explains, if you have to mix new and old materials because you've extended the path design, "Use the old brick in a medallion or other pattern to highlight its texture and color. Or do the landing with old brick, and the rest of the path with new."

Homeowner Cindy Gray gave her circular drive a twist with a recent resurfacing. "After removing the synthetic stucco and residing the house with durable HardiePlank™ shingles, we wanted the driveway to reflect the new style our home projected. With the cracks repaired, we opted for a tinted concrete with a stamped concrete border. The subtle design draws the eye from the street to the front of our home. Our neighbors tell us it makes our home a standout in the neighborhood."

Pathways and steps can be enclosed in smooth stucco walls for a formal entry rich with cultural and historical design influence.

Right: Secondary paths often come into being after someone has worn a trail through the landscaping, indicating a need for something more permanent.

A polished crab orchard patio steps up to a grass and stone path that wanders through a shade garden.
Photo by Michelle Valigursky

Slate and pea gravel offer texture and line to this home's front space.

Tinted concrete brings color to ground level.

Decking with metal and wood rails is a current solution to designing a home's approach, especially for uneven terrain.

Traditional architecture may benefit from the accent of a brick path and mulched planting beds.

The Curb Appeal Perspective: Welcome Home

With every home, physical flow of pathways and driveways is essential to achieving an optimal first impression. Sheridan Shaffer, real estate appraiser and former agent in Seattle, comments about "curable" and "incurable" defects in your home. "Curable relates to problems that can be profitably fixed and result in an increase in the value of your home," she explains. "Two hundred dollars worth of material and your own labor can turn into thousands of dollars in resale value. The good news is that most problems relating to the front of the house are curable!" She goes on to say, "A badly-laid, worn, broken front walk and cracked, oil-stained driveway, while not necessarily cheap quick fixes, are two curable elements of a home that can make a huge difference to the bottom line of your investment."

Well-maintained hardscaping won't detract from a homebuyer's first impression, but it won't necessarily wow them, either. To do that, it will have to have style, too. Greet guests with a vine-covered arbor or impressive pergola. Send them on a delightful journey through lavender and rosemary as they wind their way to the front door. Surprise them with blue stone, lava rock,

Instead of a traditional walkway approach to their home, these homeowners designed an expansive front space patio to greet guests. *Photo by Michelle Valigursky*

The patio is the perfect entertaining space surrounded by cultivated gardens. *Photo by Michelle Valigursky*

A second-story home's entry is well defined by a stone archway and slate foyer.

or cement imbedded with seashells. Your paths can blend with your overall landscape but still stand out from the norm through unexpected use of materials and direction.

Maryland Real Estate Agent Jim Southam uses his own home as an example of how to successfully meld hardscaping with a property's existing features. "We don't have brick on the home's exterior, so we knew a brick walkway wouldn't have been in keeping with our house. We are in the woods, however, with a historical stonewall on the property. To accentuate that attractive feature and to provide continuity, we chose to repeat stone elements in the yard and walkway."

There are very few houses with attractive driveways on the market at any given time, so you should expect a quick sale if yours stands out. If a full replacement project is out of your budget, you can still add pizzazz without starting from scratch. Edge it with stone or brick and surround it with planting beds so it becomes an asset to your home's façade, rather than a detractor.

Real Estate Agent's Rule: Pay attention to the appearance of your driveway and walkway and fix obvious design flaws prior to listing your home for sale. Repair safety concerns.

Hostas border stone steps for a natural edge. *Photo by Michelle Valigursky*

Chapter Eight
Lighting

Dramatic impact is achieved with wall wash lighting on this stucco home. *Photo by Michelle Valigursky*

Nothing is more alluring than the shimmer of moonlight as it plays across water, flickers across stone or dances on dewy grass. Those silvery beams are the objects of desire for many lighting designers who turn their talents toward the exterior of our homes. Using your home or yard as a blank canvas, lighting artists select key architectural or landscape features to illuminate while adding a sweep of soft light on more broad spaces such as patios and lawns. They often opt for a chiaroscuro effect, where light and dark interplay to create a complex, yet subtle result.

If outdoor lighting is done poorly, spotlights point blinding beams into home windows and entire walking areas are left in unsafe shadow. But when outdoor lighting is exceptional, an ambience is created in which hard edges are softened, drama is heightened and visitors pause to stare as they approach the home.

"Before recently, we would only occasionally do a lighting scheme as part of our landscaping jobs. Now, it's every other project," reports Landscape Designer Randy Anderson, who is pleased that more homeowners are recognizing the importance of exterior lighting. "People invest in front yard landscaping, and when it's not lit, they don't get to enjoy it as much as they could. After all, most go to work during the day and come back after dark. Without proper lighting, it's like looking into a black abyss."

In a darkened space, a single uplight on a colorful specimen tree will transform a yard into an artistic showcase.

Key architectural features may be brought into focus with down lighting.

Bright Idea: Hire a Lighting Professional

When lighting your home's exterior, you'll want to use your imagination – or tap into the imagination and skills of a qualified lighting designer. Try to recreate that feeling of being seated in a theater when the house lights go down, the curtain rises and the stage lights slowly bring into view a magnificent set. It's a breathtaking moment of awe and curiosity. That sensation is what you may hope to achieve when the sun sets and your home's lights come on for the evening.

Award winning lighting designer Doreen LeMay Madden in Belmont, Massachusetts makes the point that many people don't understand what lighting designers do. She explains their role. "In new construction and renovations, we're an important part of the design team. We integrate the important information gathered from the architect, interior designer and other professionals on the project.

"We add in the homeowners' concerns, and design a lighting scheme. This includes a detailed electrical layout with placement, loads, controls and all lighting product to be installed. The design should fulfill every need of the project from tasks, ambience, security and accents. If an individual homeowner is knowledgeable about the importance and potential of lighting, they'll also directly seek us out for expert advice." A lighting designer takes into consideration many issues for a quality lighting design, such as aesthetics of and materials used in lighting fixtures, placement of electrical connections, ease of use and maintenance, energy efficiency, controls and type of light sources to maximize both beauty and budget.

"We need to stay current on technology," LeMay Madden says. One point in fact: contrary to popular belief, modern "fluorescent lighting can be perceived as incandescent if the right source is used. It's also very energy efficient." The complexities of lighting choices are apparent in LeMay Madden's professional library. With hundreds of books devoted to lighting products, it's safe to say that an accomplished lighting designer will understand lighting intricacies that other design professionals and, of course, the average consumer may not.

For some, the thought of executing a costly lighting plan without first seeing the results can be overwhelming. "We alleviate fear up front by offering a try-before-you-buy evening demonstration," says Jeff Williams of Outdoor Lighting Perspectives of Atlanta. "We visit clients' home at night, illuminate the key features with appropriate lighting, and make adjustments before the final installation."

They advise clients to identify individual lighting and operational requirements. Once needs have been defined, they recommend a consultation by a qualified lighting designer to streamline the overall plan. A specialist will help you subtly showcase the light on your property rather than drawing attention to the source of the light.

A lighting professional may offer fixture selection not available to the general public.

A chic way to identify a property address, this light/plaque combination is both functional and attractive.

One striking light fixture can define your home's front space.

Sleek spotlights are a high style alternative to super-bright floodlights.

Warm lighting at a home's entry evokes a comfortable, inviting appearance.

Find Your Designer

A highly recognized organization for professional lighting designers is the International Association of Lighting Designers. Their website, www.fald.org. is the best place to start in your search for a lighting designer, providing contact information to professionals in your area.

This glass lamp adds a glint of polished metal against the gray-blue stone.

A pair of generously sized lamps flanks a traditional doorway.

Long, slender lamps illuminate the house numbers at this home's entry.

A single lamp not only illuminates the front steps, but also the strategically planted and sculptural greenery.

To Light or Not To Light

Lighting Designer Doreen LeMay Madden points out "A water feature such as a fountain or a goldfish pond should always be lit. It is artwork outside. And sculpture should be illuminated with three different angles of light for the most appealing effect." *Photo by Michelle Valigursky*

LeMay Madden reveals in her essay *The Psychology of Lighting*, "Lighting has two main purposes: function and impression." She gives a visual example to make her point. "Imagine two restaurant settings -- a fast-food restaurant and a romantic, elegant restaurant. Both have the same décor – blue walls, white tables and chairs, and black stone flooring. One, however, is lit with bright white, uniform lighting, while the other has soft, dim, warm glowing pools of light. Which one would be thought of for a quick inexpensive meal and which one for a relaxing, more expensive dinner? Your first impression is always determined by the lighting."

She also talks about a phenomenon called *the moth factor* that can have practical residential applications. She explains how we are attracted to light, and how we are drawn to brighter spots first. This lighting truth is used by retailers to direct attention and focus within their establishments. LeMay Madden says, "The knowledge of how and why we react to certain lighting is an important tool in lighting design."

In a home's exterior space she recommends, "Surround yourself with elements of style that reflect you and communicate a message you want others to feel." One factor often overlooked by homeowners is the fact that "interior lighting does come through at night from the exterior view. There's nothing like beautiful buildings with windows that you can see just glowing. Of course, the exterior lighting adds another layer to your interior lighting also by bringing the outdoors inside," LeMay Madden says. "I like to use layers of light because it gives the most appealing look to any type of space – different colors of light (whether natural, subtle variations of, or dramatic saturation), different intensities of light and different directions of light."

Landscape Architect Randy Anderson agrees. "Use a combination of light techniques for a subtle yet effective result," he advises. "Let light bounce around the landscape using low wattage spot and path lights, as opposed to one giant wash over the whole yard." He offers this last piece of advice to do-it-your-selfers: "Get more transformer than you need because you will lose wattage."

While solar lighting is popular with energy conservationists, the dim glow often offers far less light than is necessary to illuminate a pathway. "They often merely attract attention to themselves rather than providing adequate lighting," says Le May Madden.

Entryways become all-hours outdoor rooms with the addition of prominent lighting features and a comfortable bench or chair.
Photo by Michelle Valigursky

Lighting and windows work hand in hand to punctuate the architecture of a home. The stark geometry of this mid-century home is accentuated by indoor lighting at night.

Low-level light fixtures highlight a set of stairs which, unlit, could be a trip hazard.

Evening provides the homeowner with a fresh opportunity to wow passersby with wall wash lighting. *Photo by Scott West*

The Artistic Touch

In television productions, pale blue light is used to simulate the effect of natural moonlight. Yellow-orange incandescent light will mimic a setting sun. A rosy light will give the impression of dawn. But when lighting a house to maximize curb appeal, "Crisp pure white mercury vapor gas lights looks absolutely the best," says Jeff Williams. "Though some of our customers want to experiment with colored lenses for special occasions, the architecture stands out the best through simple application of light. We don't do much colored lighting because it can have an overpowering and garish effect."

"We recommend lighting to highlight peaks and special architectural features like keystones over windows," Williams explains. He points out that a favorite technique is "to highlight ornamental trees such as Japanese maples, crape myrtles and river birches. The variegated foliage becomes a stunning sight in the evening landscape."

"My clients rely on accent lighting to add as much drama to their exterior spaces as they do for their interior surrounds," comments Amy Novek, an ASID interior designer in New Jersey. "It's all about setting a mood. Some homes have purely functional lights, while others marry form and function with a hint of romance and personality."

LeMay Madden recalls a client who asked for subtle and natural looking exterior lighting. "We gave him a moonlighting effect, with a pale blue light source in a tree shooting down very, very softly to give the impression of a full moon."

When special occasions demand drama, look to exterior lighting as a solution. Imitate starlight by draping white twinkle lights over pergolas. Uplight columns for high impact, or install color-changing fiber optic lighting.

Some people prefer to permanently set mood-invoking lighting scenes they can recall with the touch of a button. For a high-tech approach to simplicity, LeMay Madden recommends programming a lighting keypad with different customized themes: exterior dining scene, dance party scene, low level scene, night light scene, out-of-town scene, holiday sparkle scene, etc.

A clever window art installation allows light into a neighboring yard, while also profiding privacy for the homeowner. *Photo by Jo Beserra*

Tucked among the succulents along mosaic artist Jo Beserra's front path, this canine Buddha adds an extra layer of light on special occasions. *Photo by Jo Beserra*

Lights can be mounted on posts of all varieties, including this vintage painted column.

A vintage carriage lamp reflects this historic home's era while adding panache. *Photo by Nancy Fay*

Highlight a focal point on your property to mark boundaries or draw attention to an exceptional landscaping feature. *Photo by Lisa Vail*

This home stands apart from its neighbors with a dramatic layered light look that includes moonlighting, wall wash lighting and feature lighting. *Photo by Lisa Vail*

Keep a Safe Home

While the goal of all lighting is to be aesthetically pleasing, it is also to make a home more secure. A homeowner's responsibilities extend beyond the basic bill paying, cleaning and maintaining associated with a home. Homeowners must make sure visitors will find a property safe, well lit and obstacle free.

"Attractive lights also add a big element of security when the whole front of a house is lit," according to Jeff Williams. He raises a valid question. "If a criminal is walking down the street, is he going to choose the house that is dark or is he going to approach the one that's well lit?"

Another important factor to consider when lighting your home is safety. Do you live in an area in which crime is more prevalent? Motion sensor lights will add peace of mind as well as practicality. "Aim them at a pathway or shrubbery where people could hide. A little light goes a long way at night, so low wattage may work just fine for your situation," LeMay Madden recommends.

Your home's street entrance should be highly visible, with house numbers clearly defined. The driveway should be sufficiently bright for a visitor to make the way to an illuminated pathway. Adequate lighting on walking surfaces lessens the likelihood of visitors tripping on a raised tree root or falling on slick hardscaping. Other functional lights include those that enable you to see the door lock or alarm keypad.

"Some people think if you over-light and flood the whole house that it's great for security. But having too much light can be as bad as having no light as far as safety from intruders," according to LeMay Madden. "Think of it this way. The intruder has a plan. You don't. You're just coming home, and you're in bright light fumbling with your handbag and house keys. He can see everything you're doing. Your eye is not able to adapt to his whereabouts because of the excessively bright light. That can be just as dangerous as a too-dark setting. Balance is the best solution."

Emergency responders need to be able to identify a property address at a glance. Keep house numbers well lit and clearly visible for your own safety.

Architectural style can be reflected in lighting choice, as with this clean-lined light style for a Craftsman home.

Grassy stone steps are navigable at night when illuminated by low-voltage lights. *Photo by Lisa Vail*

A single lamp can make an artistic statement at night. *Photo by Lisa Vail*

The Curb Appeal Perspective: Be Dramatic

partner back to see. Since this usually happens at night after work, the exterior front lighting of a home is critical to it showing well."

Caldwell goes on to say, "Exterior lighting is important. Even though most agents do their showings during the day, many eager buyers will drive by for a second time at night."

Melissa Atherholt, a Maryland real estate agent, agrees. "For night showings, two simple spotlights on the house add so much." While evening lighting is a magnificent addition to any home, she shares a pennywise recommendation. "When your house is for sale and you don't have an extensive outdoor lighting scheme, invest 20 dollars in a pair of portable outdoor floodlights available from any home improvement center. They're cheap, they're temporary, but when you shine one on your front door you add instant impact. Add a second spotlight to highlight a terrific landscaping element such as a stone waterfall. Or, uplight a single tree for drama on the home's front space."

Don't worry when an illuminated red maple or other deciduous tree sheds its leaves. As LeMay Madden explains, "Trees are just as beautiful in winter. They become sculptural as the branches stand out in stark relief against the light."

Real Estate Agent's Rule: Always replace burned out bulbs and broken fixtures to avoid the haunted house effect. Spooky isn't saleable.

When choosing light fixtures, consider scale and proportion as well as light output.

Buyers love homes with pizzazz. And whether flamboyant or reserved, they love homes with great night lighting. "It's about drama. The first impression a home makes is what the buyer will come back to when he's making a decision," says Colleen Geppi, a real estate agent in Frederick, Maryland. "When they love the inside, knowing the outside is showcased with professional lighting just seems to cement the deal."

Real Estate Agent Michael Caldwell makes another point. "Because life in Los Angeles tends to be fast-paced, couples in house-hunting mode often have to split responsibilities. One person will preview 10 houses and pick out the best options to bring their

Atlanta Blacksmith Thomas Boston Clarkson created this iron and stone outdoor fireplace for his home's front space. "In my metalwork, I use a variety of techniques specific to blacksmithing – striking, piercing, bending, twisting and forge welding to produce joinery and textures that express harmony of design and function," he explains. "The result is an artful balance of plasticity and thoughtful spontaneity." *Photo by Louis Cahill*

The smooth stucco boundary or garden wall is a common feature in California's Spanish Colonial Revival and Mexican architecture.

Chapter Nine
Setting Boundaries

A raised ranch is bounded by a neat picket fence and retro-inspired metal neighbor gate.

reveal fences, hedges, rock walls and tree lines. To each of us, the definition of a boundary will differ only by materials or the purpose for which the boundary is created. We need property boundaries to increase privacy and security, screen unsightly views and noise, define the walls of a garden room, or keep pets and children out of harm's way. Still others want boundaries to add definition to a house and yard.

Architect Miri Lerner never puts high fences or courtyard walls around her properties. She "hates the idea of fortressing" and contends that a low wall or fence is suitable because its purpose is to define space, rather than fortress the inhabitants in.

Harmony with the property's surrounds is very important. Always discuss a new fence or hedge with neighbors if it will adjoin their property in any way – visual or physical.

Fencing takes a new slant with this linear fence in front of a California modern residence.

We all want to protect our own corner of the world. We enclose rooms with doors. We further define homes by windows, walls and roofs. It's only natural that we seek to contain property as well.

The world has seen its great examples of divisive boundaries. The Great Wall of China and the Berlin Wall originally were built to confine citizens and keep out opponents, but remained standing as symbolic representations of political history. In medieval times, Europeans walled their cities and castle keeps as a first line of defense. In less turbulent eras, the English and French enclosed their mazes and formal gardens with sculpted hedges.

The idea is, and has always been, to respect personal space. Today, a drive through any given city will

In Bounds or Out?

It's time to go back to basics. Before we can begin any discussion of fencing and boundary types, we must address the most crucial element in your planning process: identifying your exact property boundaries. While it may be tempting to guesstimate the lines, it can be far less costly to invest in a professional survey of your land before any constructive boundary is built or planted. We could name multiple lawsuits that have been the direct result of homeowners' incorrect assumptions. In these cases, the financial ramifications of assumptions far surpassed the few hundred dollars it might have cost for a survey.

Before you construct a boundary, take heed of community limitations. Most property lines are restricted by setback requirements that dictate how close to the street you can set a fence line, or if you can at all. Similarly, setbacks affect the shared edges of your property and your neighbors, and can determine which way a fence should face. Height restrictions and picket spacing requirements may also affect your decision. Consult your local zoning office for specific restrictions before making a costly mistake. Also ask if a building permit is required before construction.

If you plan to reduce or increase plantings at a property's edge, neighborly approval is always welcome and is sometimes mandated. Homeowners with historic homes also face adherence to strict guidelines imposed by historical associations.

This Japanese–inspired home is framed by a simple wood perimeter fence in deference to the home's architectural style. *Photo by Lisa Vail*

A decorative boundary fence adds a geometric edge to a hedgerow of blooming azaleas.

But let the property owner beware: the local zoning board may not be the only source to consult. In addition, be sure to check with your homeowner's association's architectural review committee when appropriate. These committees often require neighbors' signatures on detailed diagrams of the intended changes.

Often, homeowners think of gates merely as functional entry points at the beginning of a path or a segue to the backyard at the end of a drive. Blacksmith Thomas Boston Clarkson created this gate for a larger purpose. "Gates can be sculptural works of art that provide access to places beyond. As a standalone sculpture, the gate acts as a metaphor for invitation." *Photo by Louis Cahill*

The basic picket fence gets a facelift with fleur de lis tops. *Photo by Lisa Vail*

The exuberant array of aloe and flaxes obscure what would otherwise be an imposing courtyard wall.

This fence was created using a centuries-old technique called wattling in which twigs are woven between stakes. *Photo by Michelle Valigursky*

A circular design was repeated often in this iron fencing for an older city home. *Photo by Michelle Valigursky*

As in the children's classic *The Secret Garden*, gates beckon entry to the mysterious garden beyond. *Photo by Michelle Valigursky*

Picket, Stone or Privet?

Boundary selection lends a first impression about the type of property that lies within. But, as with all other aesthetically pleasing curb appeal decisions, form and function often go hand in hand.

In one of her renovations, Author Lisa Vail created an informal, natural fence in front of the home by letting existing bushes grow out and filling in with ornamental grasses, rosemary, lavender and other drought-tolerant plantings for a difficult to water outer area. "A short time later when we adopted rescue dogs, this natural fencing no longer worked for us. It is important to periodically reassess fencing needs."

Necessity, too, can dictate boundary choice. Lisa says, "At a corner lot home we renovated, we faced a very busy street along one side of the property. We hired a craftsman well known for his simple yet beautiful redwood fences to create a tongue and groove 6-foot tall fence to block the noise and sightline of the street. Because sound bounces off solid surfaces, the fence had to be tongue-and-groove with no gaps between the boards to achieve the full sound barrier effect."

Once function is addressed, the elements of design come into play. Consider all varieties of plantings to soften a landscape and highlight the architectural value of your fencing choice. Fencing can also be used as a decorative accent, rather than an impenetrable boundary. Sections of fence can highlight a patio or deck, or surround a play area beneath a tree. Think of your landscape as usable living space, and measure how partial fences or walls may help you carve out the rooms you desire.

Erosion control is a key goal for retaining walls. Stacked stone and Belgian block are excellent materials for creating a boundary with a purpose.

The acrylic panels in this modern redwood fence give the impression of a shoji screen.

Property can be effectively bounded by live fences in which plants are encouraged to grow together for privacy.

The tongue-and-groove building technique, in which there are no gaps between planks, will act as an effective sound barrier when needed.

Trade Secret

An off-the-shelf picket fence was painted the same creamy green of this renovated bungalow's trim, then heavily planted to give it a "been there forever" look. *Photo by Costa Singer*

All fences contain the same basic component parts: vertical posts, horizontal rails and decorative elements that surface the fence. Because they are forced to withstand assault by the elements, coating a fence with varnish or polyurethane is never recommended. Pressure treated lumber is almost a necessity for durability.

Since no one wants to be Tom Sawyer with a huge fence to sand, scrape and paint, what's the best-applied finish to consider for the least amount of long-term maintenance? Semi-transparent stain. The most high maintenance finish? Flat white paint. The most cost efficient and time sensitive finish? Pre-fabricated, pre-finished plastic composite. If you are going to paint, always prime bare wood and apply top quality exterior paint.

This casual wall of shrubbery is intended to define this home's front space rather than act as a true barrier.

Creeping fig frames a simple yet elegant courtyard gate. *Photo by Michelle Valigursky*

Give Typical a Twist

As we've said many times, traditional choices don't have to be predictable. Lisa Vail recalls, "In the front yard of one of my cottage-style renovations, we ripped out the existing chain link fence and replaced it with a pre-fab picket fence from Lowe's. As a twist to the typical white picket fence, we added a dab of soft creamy green to complement the house trim. The new fence really said artistic cottage, which was exactly the image we were trying to sell for the house." She continues, "One side of the front yard revealed a view of the neighbors' unattractive driveway. To block it out, we erected a framed lattice panel tall enough to screen the view then planted a honeysuckle vine to fill in. By using the lattice, rather than constructing a solid barrier, we kept the small front yard from feeling claustrophobic."

Recycling, too, can lead to clever interpretations. Lisa used broken concrete from a jack-hammered patio instead of stone to make a 3-foot stacked wall. "We filled crevices with soil and planted succulents to grow out of the wall."

Nail heads, iron trim and a color-washing technique turns a simple courtyard door into a showcase piece.

A locally-crafted gate is a delightful departure from the norm.

Airy spindles make this gate more approachable than a solid version.

Regional Materials

What's natural to your area? Lava rock? Coral? Cedar? Stone? Using regionally available materials for boundaries makes great financial and design sense.

In New England, Real Estate Broker Terry Keegan points out that "Visitors to our area are amazed at the quantity of stone. Drive along the streets and look through the woods and you'll see beautiful stone walls running between the properties." He adds, "In the old days, they used to give away stone. Now it's a valuable commodity."

In semi-tropical climes such as south Florida where plant life thrives, "Ficus trees are the number one formal landscaping hedge," according to Real Estate Agent Bob Bourne. "When trimmed weekly, they can be shaped with archways to walk under. People also use areca palms as a dense hedge. They're quick growing, send up new shoots from the bottom and provide natural movement." Bourne notes that his clients have found that "orange jasmine, though limited in lifespan and somewhat woody in the formative stages, offers beautiful fragrance in a hedge."

In the Pacific Northwest, Real Estate Agent Pam Brossard says "blooming heather offers a punch of beautiful purple and comes into flower when other plants won't. People plant this to create lovely free-flowing boundaries." In the Southwest, Real Estate Agent Kelly Thate points out that mountain laurel and lantana are popular choices for hedges because of their ability to be shaped. In the Southeast, long lines of dense Leland Cypress trees or quick-growing red tips effectively create separation between one property and the next.

Natural elements over man-made bases are also common around the country. Bourne cites examples of poured concrete or cinder block walls skimmed in a veneer of coral stone, stucco or brick. On Maui, Real Estate Agent Janice Goodnight explains that lava rock and blue rock are key design components in both retaining and decorative walls.

Mexican bush sage atop a stacked stone retaining wall thrive at the entrance of this Mission-style hacienda.

Tuck plants into crevices of rock and stone walls; in time, they will naturalize and fill the gaps with color, texture and scent. *Photo by Lisa Vail*

Live fencing can be achieved with many low maintenance plants including ficus, hedge roses and more.

Soft grasses create an effective border at a property edge. *Photo by Michelle Valigursky*

Western Red Cedar is popular in north and southwestern United States
for its inherent beauty and natural oils that repel insects.

The Curb Appeal Perspective: Property Lines

Landscape elements can accent a wall, offering both color and design in an artistic presentation of plant life.

Homeowners often inadvertently turn off buyers with fence, wall, and hedging selections. Jim Southam, a real estate veteran in Maryland, has seen his share of poor boundary choices. He contends that clients need to consider the impact of their decisions. "If your property is wooded, for instance, minimize attention to your fence. You're in a situation that's crying out for nature to be kept whole." In such cases, Southam recommends, "Keep the color palette as natural as possible. If wire is a necessity, use a green version with split rail to blend in with the natural environment."

Undersized trees and plants meant for screening concern Southam, as they also do Austin Real Estate Agent Kelly Thate. Southam says, "When I recommend my clients plant a border to block out unsightly views, I'm not talking about gallon bucket plants." Thate agrees. "For drama and impact, buy plants of substantial size."

Los Angeles Real Estate Agents Katherine Davis and Michael Caldwell dislike it when people put their tall fence or hedge right up to the sidewalk or property line. Davis explains, "Leave space for plantings on the outside to soften the effect."

Caldwell adds to this, pointing out that really high, solid walls make the front of the home feel unapproachable. To counteract this negative first impression, he suggests softening the mood at the entrance with an attractive light fixture, an artistic plaque, and really nice street numbers. "And make sure visitors know how to contact you once they've arrived. A call system, well lit and easy to find, is really helpful in this situation."

And lastly, everyone agreed that boundary choices needed to be in keeping with the style and size of the home. Always look to your home's architecture for cues on fence styling and proportion. And never, ever should chain link be considered an option.

Real Estate Agent's Rule: Whatever boundary you choose to use, do it well and do it to the right scale. When in doubt, consult an architect or landscape planner for guidance.

Decorative wooden gates elevate beyond function to an art form when given a color wash.

Opposite page:
Bamboo is safely contained to provide a stalky screen to edge a sidewalk.

A stately copper obelisk takes on an oxidized patina over time. *Photo by Michelle Valigursky*

Chapter Ten
The Finishing Touch

Like jewelry on an elegant party dress, or the just-right footwear that pulls together an everyday ensemble, home and garden accessories add the finishing touch to a home's front space. They are the bits of glam that stimulate the senses and exist merely to delight – Victorian gazing balls, fountains, fire pits and wind chimes. They're also the worker-bees of exterior life – mailboxes, birdbaths and house numbers.

Inside your home you'll find a treasure trove of accessories lovingly selected – mementos purchased on jaunts around the world, keepsakes handed down through the generations, and *objets d'art* that enhance the décor to make a personal statement. Without these touches, your home's interior would feel lifeless, uninhabited, and expressionless. But homeowners often forget the exterior of the home deserves the same level of detail. Without the right accessories, it's just not complete.

The best front-of-the-home accents perform double duty – offering function as well as finesse. They receive our mail while enhancing architectural style. Shelter our avian friends while introducing a garden theme. Mask an unwanted view while enticing visitors with our artistic expression. By applying the same design principles used in creating a great outfit or a great room, you can use accessories to provide those personal touches that define an exceptional home.

Fountains, both classical and modern, can be the majestic focal point of your front space.

An avant garde sculpture delights and surprises visitors to this traditional home.

Sharp Focus

A bas-relief plaque is a unique way to add artistry to the front of your home, whether it's propped up in a garden bed or hung by the front door. *Photo by Michelle Valigursky*

A classical relief framing the house numbers on this city home evoke another time and place. *Photo by Michelle Valigursky*

Every masterpiece has a focal point. So, too, should your home's front view. When you look upon your property, to which element is the eye immediately drawn? If your focus is pulled in different directions, or worse yet, finds nothing interesting at all to light upon, it's time to rethink your accessory situation.

When using accessories to enhance your home's curb appeal, Designer and Mosaic Artist Jo Beserra recommends a sequential approach from the beginning of the design process. "Determine what will be the focal point of the space first then use that special piece to drive the rest of the design concept. For example, if you are featuring a sculpture or a fountain in your front garden or courtyard, create a seating area from which to view it and an arbor or pathway leading you to it."

Beserra calls upon his fine arts background to visualize accessory placement. "Space relations in a yard are no different than in any other type of design or artwork. You put shapes and objects together to achieve contrast, visual depth and surprise."

In her book *Garden Ornament*, Linda Joan Smith offers her own insights into the role of accessories. She says, an ornament "brings focus to the landscaping and directs the eye of the onlooker just where it's meant to go. Such ornament can expand or shrink the perceived size of the garden space, shape the path one takes, influence where one pauses, and lure one's gaze away from garden flaws."

Just as a room full of knick-knacks covering every surface overwhelms, too many details will also clutter an exterior landscape. Remember, your goal should be to showcase your home, not detract from it. Says Beserra: "It's much more fun when things are revealed slowly, as opposed to a full frontal assault of tchotchkes. Let the sound of a fountain draw the visitor down the path and let them have the pleasure of discovering it. Make a strong impact with one exquisite accessory placed well."

This sculpture is so life-like, a visitor might need a second glance. *Photo by Michelle Valigursky*

Quiet vignettes of serenity are welcome in any front space.
Photo by Michelle Valigursky

A Buddha statue along a Zen-Modern front walk invites us to contemplate the cosmos with him.

While high-tech replacements exist to keep squirrels at bay, some people prefer the simplicity of a rustic wooden birdhouse mounted on a fence post.

Function or statement? Why not have both, like this artisan-crafted mailbox?

The color, material and theme of this mailbox was inspired by the house itself.

An interesting pot makes an inexpensive focal point in a landscape bed. This is a good use for broken pottery, as well. *Photo by Lisa Vail*

The statue, perfectly framed by a vine-covered arbor, beckons us to explore the many layers of interest in this side yard garden. *Photo by Michelle Valigursky*

Form vs. Function

What are your goals for accessorizing your front space? Do you want to establish poetic elements of beauty, or do you need to maximize utility with objects that serve a purpose beyond being eye-catching?

Beserra recalls a form vs. function problem he recently solved. "My own yard butts up against my neighbor's. Where they need light, I need privacy. I devised a privacy screen from a salvaged window. With textured glass and faux finishing, I satisfied both needs and offered visitors to my home something beautiful."

So how do you cope with pesky front yard necessities like garden hoses? One perfectly aesthetic solution is to abandon the garden hose altogether in favor of more efficient drip systems and automatic sprinklers. If you prefer sprinklers, consider that water flows beautifully from lovely copper sculptures that act both as ornamental art and functional irrigation. These sprinklers can be yard mounted at varying heights for six to 40 feet of watering coverage.

Architect David Sharff recommends using attractive built-in porch benches for storing cushions and garden miscellany. "Consider your home's architecture when choosing storage options. We've custom built solutions for historic properties using bead board to complement the exterior and blend with the home's lines."

We've seen many otherwise perfect home fronts marred by a left-out garden hose. Keep it tidy yet still at hand with a decorative mount. *Photo by Michelle Valigursky*

Stepping stones leading to a sitting area in Master Garderner Ellen Ungashick's front garden marries artistry with utility.

Trade Secret:

Just like our interior designs, accessories help establish the concept of our outside spaces. A serene, Japanese-inspired theme will be supported by a perfectly placed Buddha, wind chimes, and a tsukubai bamboo and stone water fountain traditionally found in tea gardens. Likewise, two classically-inspired urns flanking the front door in perfect symmetry will set an elegant and formal tone to a home.

What about gutter systems? Nothing can disrupt the clean lines of a contemporary home more than obtrusive metal downspouts. The answer for many designers is the rain chain. The Japanese have relied on rain chains for hundreds of years to collect rainwater, yet this ancient custom has only come into popularity in the United States in the last few years. Says Author Lisa Vail, "Many top architects are specifying rain chains for their ecologically responsible properties. Rather than diverting rainwater away from the house and into storm drains, water flows over sculptural copper chains into catch basins to be used in gardening or into rain gardens where it is filtered and absorbed back into the ground. Rain chains are an attractive rain harvesting and stormwater management solutions."

Rain chains are an unobtrusive way to deal with a necessity like drainage.

Brush Strokes

Artist Jo Beserra's paintings of clouds and sky gives depth and interest to an expansive blank space. *Photo by Jo Beserra*

Imagine sipping wine while gazing at a sweeping view of rows of glistening grapevines. Perhaps you see a forbidden glimpse inside a sunroom where a lazy cat sleeps. Or maybe you envision a beckoning entry into a shadowed garden.

You can have it all and more with *trompe l'oeil*. Fool the eye. It's the mural artist's trick of setting a scene with the mystery and inspiration of paint and it's been around since 400 B.C. when the Greeks and Romans embellished the walls of their homes. Architect Leone Alberti claimed the technique offered "a window into space." Today, urban artists reclaim graffiti-stained walls with expressions of community and spirituality, changing the high-rise landscapes of our nation's largest cities.

These same *trompe l'oeil* techniques have residential applications. Jo Beserra learned the technique while set painting. "Working on scenery made me aware that you can create any kind of aesthetic for your home with paint. It's the most inexpensive way to do something lush and wonderful with incredible dramatic impact. And it's especially effective outdoors."

Jack Pabis is a Maryland muralist whose imagination takes shape through vivid brush strokes and splashes of color. "Murals offer the illusion of something more. On the surface of a garage door, for example, my clients want rose gardens, crumbling Roman ruins, or open windows. There is no limit to what we can create."

Pabis explains the technique. "The simplest outdoor murals are usually done in exterior oil-based house paint. When painting over a porous surface such as brick or concrete, we treat the area in advance of the mural creation. A homeowner can extend the life of a mural by choosing a location with indirect light and sealing it periodically with a non-yellowing oil-based or polyurethane varnish."

Murals and other outdoor paint effects, like this one by trompe l'oeil master William Cochran, let the homeowner visit imaginary worlds every day. *Photo by Michelle Valigursky*

A Bit of Whimsy

"The furnishing of a garden, like that of a house, happens over time," says Linda Joan Smith in her book *Garden Ornament*. Instead of filling a cart at the local superstore, she contends, "better to wait for the perfect ornament to come along at a tag sale or antique show, on a trip to Holland or Africa, or at a nursery in a neighboring town. Then leave room in your garden for unexpected finds."

Those garden items need not be serious, such as the whimsical and colorful hand-blown gazing balls enjoying popularity these days. Some have called them witch balls or globes of happiness, but as Sir Francis Bacon stated, "a proper garden would have round colored balls for the sun to play upon." In 1612, an Italian priest named Antonio Neri named them "spheres of light." Superstition tells that they ward off evil and bad fortune, and in exchange, provide the owner with happiness. In Victorian times, blue or gold gazing balls were hung in front room windows to repel witches.

Shops today feature gazing balls in a kaleidoscope of colors and resin or cement foundation stands. These colorful accents add reflection and prominence to any planting bed or garden area, whether suspended from trees like holiday ornaments or tucked into a planting bed awaiting discovery.

Don't settle for ordinary when unique is so much more satisfying for the creative spirit.

A teacup birdbath amid the daisies reminds visitors to take pause and enjoy a leisurely stroll.

Glass mosaic house numbers inset in the front sidewalk announce your arrival.

A copper spider in the front garden continues the whimsical bug theme.

Choose pieces that reflect your personality or move you emotionally. This alligator can always elicit a laugh. *Photo by Lisa Vail*

Opposite page:
Playful architecture calls for playful accessories.

Water, Water Everywhere

Nothing holds more universal appeal than the sound and sight of running water. The soothing influence it has on us can't be definitively explained. Perhaps it goes back to our primal human desire to live near water, on which man is dependent for survival, or a physiological syncopation with our own inner H2O. Or, it could simply be a reminder of carefree days at the beach or wading through a forest creek.

"There is no front garden or entryway that won't benefit from a water feature. Not a day goes by that we aren't installing one for a client, "says Landscape Designer Randy Anderson. The most elaborate and most expensive are boulder waterfall designs, but he assures that a water feature is possible on any budget. "Even a birdbath can act as a water feature because of the animation when birds splash."

With a kit from your local garden supply store, create a fountain out of any vessel you'd like. Water spilling from a large urn into a bed of pebbles (the water re-circulates through tubing in a watertight reservoir underneath) makes a simple yet striking statement. Be sure to seal porous, unglazed pots to prevent leakage. Consider the location from inside the home and out to maximize enjoyment. And don't forget to illuminate your water feature for added drama.

This classically-designed cast iron fountain also serves as a birdbath. *Photo by Michelle Valigursky*

In Jo Beserra's front garden, the mosaic fountain pays homage to his grandmother, whose collection of Presidential plates was the impetus for this functional work of art. *Photo by Jo Beserra*

The Curb Appeal Perspective:
Pink Flamingos and Grinning Gnomes

Though we know one man's trash is another man's treasure, one pink flamingo in the yard is probably better than a flock, and one grinning gnome is more than enough to peek from the boxwood hedge.

Yard art is a maybe at best from the real estate agent's perspective. When advising our clients on how to boost the home's curb space appeal, we repeat the mantra made famous by 20th century architect Mies van der Rohe. "Less is more." The emphasis should rest on the landscaping and the spatial arrangement of greenery and free space. A visitor's eye should be able to absorb your home's architectural presence.

Unraveled garden hoses, abandoned yard tools and miscellaneous debris should not clutter a home's front space. And clusters of marginally tasteful figurines will most likely send buyers racing to the next listing. That doesn't mean homeowners shouldn't feel free to express themselves outdoors. To keep the mood light and inviting, Real Estate Agent Michael Caldwell

The formality of the symmetrically placed urns is downplayed by the casual reed basket for a welcoming presentation.

Real estate agent Michael Caldwell suggests placing a fanciful object near the front door to put homebuyers in a good mood to view your home.

suggests introducing a single touch of whimsy for a bit of fun. "When staging my properties, I place a teeny birdhouse by the door to make people smile." Form and function often overlap, as in the case of artistic water features. Caldwell explains, "Fountains out front can diminish the sound of traffic or of playing children at school recess down the street. The fountain creates a white noise. When you hear and see running water, your mind displaces the other, unwanted sounds."

Real Estate Agent's Rule: Think clean. Think organized. Think visual continuity with a creative spark. And if you need to, choose your favorite lawn gnome and send his other gnome buddies on a journey to the backyard.

Bibliography

Though hundreds of books, magazines, and websites served as research tools for the authors, the following books were quite informative and inspirational:

Burnett, Frances Hodgson. *The Secret Garden*, W.W. Norton, 2007.

Dolan, Michael. *The American Porch: An Informal History of an Informal Place*, The Lyons Press, 2004.

Jacobs, Jane. *The Death and Life of Great American Cities*, Modern Library Series, 1993.

Kahn, Renee and Meagher, Ellen. *Preserving Porches*, Henry Holt and Co., 1990.

Nash, George. *Renovating Old Houses: Bringing New Life to Vintage Homes*, Taunton Press, 2003.

Obolensky, Kira. *Garage: Reinventing the Place We Park*, Taunton, 2003.

Primeau, Liz. *Front Yard Gardens: Growing More than Grass*, Firefly Books, 2003.

Prizeman, John. *Your House: The Outside View*, International Specialized Book Service, 1986.

Smith, Linda Joan. *Garden Ornament*, Workman Publishing, 1998.

Versaci, Russell. *Creating a New Old House: Yesterday's Character for Today's Home*, Taunton, 2007

Index